The Gathering of Friends

Apprentices have asked me, what is the most exalted peak of cuisine?
Is it the freshest ingredients, the most complex flavours? Is it the rustic, or the rare?
The peak is neither eating nor cooking, but the giving and sharing of food.
Great food should never be taken alone. What pleasure can a man take in fine
cuisine unless he invites cherished friends, counts the days until the banquet,
and composes an anticipatory poem for his letter of invitation?

– Liang Wei, The Last Chinese Chef, pub. Peking, 1925

❧ Michelle Huxtable ❧

Photography by Megan Cornelius Turley

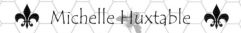

❦ *Introduction* ❦

*G*rowing up in the early 1960's, I fondly remember watching my mother in the kitchen creatively prepare our meals. I loved the way she involved her children in preparations, allowing us to cook with her. She patiently taught us the intricacies of cuisine and the proper way to dress a table. I remember anticipating a variety of my favorite dishes that my mother created. She had a masterful way of making all of us feel loved and important. Every meal seemed effortless as she derived great joy from gathering her family around her. I now realize that *food* was indeed her *love language*, and that we share a longing to surround ourselves with, and feed, those we love.

Our experience as a family, gathering around the table, visiting, discussing our worlds, has always made me feel safe. As children, we eagerly awaited our father's return from a long day and the chance we then had to gather together. My parents operated like clockwork. Dinner was scheduled at 5:30, and my mother was prepared with the most wonderful meals: oven baked breads, homemade pastries, succulent fruits and jams from our fruit trees, fresh corn, green beans, and baked potatoes, all things harvested from our garden. And yet, sometimes we feasted on toasted tomato sandwiches. At one time we had a garden that was a full acre. I remember looking down those long rows, as we began to weed, thinking we would never get to the end. But we did, and when we gathered, we enjoyed the fruits of our labors.

One of my earliest memories as a child was my mother's compassionate generosity. In those early years, we lived in the city of Toronto. Like most women in that era, my mother didn't drive, so we took the subway everywhere we needed to go. My father went off to work every day and would leave my mother a five-dollar bill to go to the market and to shop for odds and ends. We lived in a beautiful home on a graceful street. As was custom in those days, we frequently had people come to the back door in need of a meal, or looking for odd jobs to help them in a time of distress.

There was one man in particular, for whom my mother had great compassion. He began coming every three to four weeks, and for a reason initially unknown to my siblings and me, my mother would give him the entire five dollars. He never asked for the money, but she sensed that he needed it much more than we did.

One fall day, while he was finishing an odd job, mother asked him if he was going to be in town for Thanksgiving. He said that he was, and she casually invited him to celebrate with us. He looked mildly surprised, yet pleased, and said he would be honored to come.

Thanksgiving day arrived. In the early afternoon, a showered, clean-shaven, and nearly unrecognizable friend, came to our door. He was wearing new clothes, gently used from Goodwill, and appeared so happy to be there. I marvel now at the compassion my parents showed for those less fortunate than we. He was treated with great kindness and respect, indeed as if he were king for a day!

As the gathering came to a close, my tenderhearted father offered to drive him home, which he graciously accepted. He requested that my father drop him off in the heart of the city. It was quite clear that he was homeless. My father dropped him off and watched him disappear nobly into the darkness. Our parents always taught us the importance of treating others with respect, regardless of circumstance.

A close friend's mother always says, "True character is revealed by how you treat those who serve you." I have been surrounded all my life by gracious examples of those that understand and live this principle.

I have thought often of that and many other generous acts of kindness. I thank my parents and others for their goodness. On the previous page, you can see a celebration in their honor: a collection of pictures of my father and mother on their wedding day, old photos of my grandparents and great grandparents, and one of my daughter's wedding photos. These memories, set in their honor, amongst their beautiful dishes and stem wear, dress a table.

My mother derived great pleasure in making her home a graceful haven, where everyone who entered always felt welcome. Making food her *love language* began a tradition that I have tried to share with my own children, grandchildren, and friends. The Gathering of Friends Volume Two is an expression of my desire to carry this tradition forward.

Michelle

www.thegatheringoffriends.com

The
Gathering
of Friends ⚜

is a registered trademark of Clarenden Woods, LLC.

The Gathering of Friends volume two. 1st edition
Library of Congress Control Number: 2009933057
ISBN: 978-0-9816986-1-8

Second Edition
10 9 8 7 6 5 4 3 2

Editor in Chief: Abby Jane Green
Executive Editor: Michelle Huxtable
Graphic Designer: Brayden Iwasaki

Published by Clarenden Woods, LLC.

❧ Contents ❧

-CHAPTER ONE-

Gatherings: Week One - 11

-CHAPTER TWO-

Gatherings: Week Two - 37

-CHAPTER THREE-

Gatherings: Week Three - 63

-CHAPTER FOUR-

Gatherings: Week Four - 86

-CHAPTER FIVE-

Gatherings: Week Five - 110

-CHAPTER SIX-

Effortless Dishes - 134

-CHAPTER SEVEN-

Savory Beginnings - 148

-CHAPTER EIGHT-

Wholesome Soups from the Kitchen-162

-CHAPTER NINE-

Garden Fresh Salads - 176

-CHAPTER TEN-

Enchanting Desserts - 190

Preface

We believe in the inevitable success of a child who gathers with family and frequently shares a meal. We hear of top Fortune 500 companies whose chief officers share a common thread: eating dinner as a family at least three times a week. As my own child rearing years continue, mealtime is my solace. Gathering together at mealtime deepens our understanding and compassion for each other. It suggests we look at one another, drawing us closer as we communicate and contemplate.

Often, added guests dish up healthy doses of much needed wisdom and advice. Although I couldn't give my children all I desired, I could feed them daily, break bread, give thanks for them, thus, instilling confidence and refined attributes. Gathering together creates cherished memories; one meal at a time, as our lives unfold around the table. This has proven to give them much more than I ever dreamed possible.

My hope is this book may empower the reader with simple ideas to enhance mealtime in your home, around your circle of influence of family and friends. Having a meal plan is half the battle.

Gathering your family, making friends your family and family your friends is certainly celebrating life.

For years I have collected beehives: all shapes and sizes. I'm fascinated at the whole social structure of the hive. I believe home is very much like the beehive: where hard work produces the sweetest of rewards.

Bee Joyful!

CHAPTER ONE

Gatherings

Week One
Evening One

Crispy Chicken Avocado Tacos

Tender pieces of chicken breast sautéed crisp in a coating of crushed corn tortilla chips, served with a generous slice of ripe green avocado and crunchy shredded cabbage in a fresh corn tortilla, finished with a drizzle of Spicy Salsa Ranch and a sprinkling of garden fresh cilantro leaves

Spicy Salsa Ranch

Creamy ranch dressing swirled in spicy fresh tomato and jalapeño salsa, Ole'

Shrimp Cauliflower Salad

Sweet tender baby shrimp, crunchy pieces of fresh cauliflower and crisp green beans tossed in a cool lime fresh dill dressing

Baja Steamed Rice

Bright red and yellow sweet peppers, tender green onions and plump ripe tomatoes folded into fluffy cumin infused rice

Cornbread From the Heart

Sweet, satisfying heart-shaped cornbread muffins topped with sugary kernels of lightly sautéed fresh corn

Crispy Chicken Avocado Tacos ⚜

- 4 tender chicken breasts
  boneless, skinless
- 2 eggs
- 2 c. flour
- 1½ tsp. salt
- 1½ tsp. fresh ground pepper
- 2 c. crushed tortilla chips
- ½ c. vegetable oil
  extra virgin olive oil
- 18 sm. fresh corn tortillas
- 2 c. shredded cabbage
- 2 med. ripe avocado
- ½ c. fresh cilantro, gently chopped

Slice chicken breasts into strips, dip in beaten eggs and then into flour, salt and pepper mixture. Place floured chicken pieces back into the egg mixture and roll chicken strip in finely crushed tortilla chips. In a medium hot skillet lightly sauté chicken strips in vegetable oil. Drizzle olive oil in skillet and lightly fry corn tortillas until golden. Do not over cook. Place chicken strips in tortilla, add shredded cabbage and a generous slice of avocado, finish with Spicy Salsa Ranch topped with fresh cilantro.

Spicy Salsa Ranch ⚜

- 1 c. milk
- 1 tbsp. white vinegar or lemon juice
- 1 c. mayonnaise
- 1 tbsp. Homemade Dry Ranch Dressing Mix (pg. 188)
  or 1 pkg. Ranch Dressing Mix
- 1 c. fresh salsa

Combine lemon juice or vinegar with milk. Fold in mayonnaise and dry ranch mix. Add salsa and chill.

Baja Steamed Rice

3 c. white rice
½ tsp. ground cumin
1 tsp. salt

1 med. yellow bell pepper
1 med. red bell pepper

1 plump ripe tomato
4 young green onions

Cook rice as per instructions on package adding cumin to the water. Just before serving, fold in finely chopped vegetables, salt and fresh ground pepper to taste

Shrimp Cauliflower Salad

In a 4 qt. soup pot bring 1 qt. of water to a boil. Break cauliflower into pieces and blanch for 2 minutes, add green beans and cook for an additional 1 minute in the same pot. Pour into a strainer and rinse with cold water. In a large salad bowl, whisk mayonnaise, fresh lime, minced fresh dill and diced green onions. Fold in blanched vegetables and bay shrimp. Salt and pepper to taste. Chill.

1 head of cauliflower
2½ c. slim green beans, chopped
¾ c. mayonnaise
juice of 1 freshly squeezed lime
⅓ c. fresh dill, gently minced
4 green onions
2 lb. cooked bay shrimp
salt and pepper

Cornbread From the Heart ⚜

1 ear of corn
½ c. + 1 tbsp. butter
⅔ c. + 1 tbsp. sugar
2 eggs
1 c. buttermilk
½ tsp. baking soda

1 c. cornmeal
1 c. flour
½ tsp. salt

Preheat oven to 375°. Sauté fresh cut corn in 1 tbsp. butter and 1 tbsp. sugar in frying pan. Brown corn in the butter for 2-3 minutes and set aside. In a medium size bowl melt ½ c. creamy butter in microwave and stir in ⅔ c. sugar. Mix in eggs and beat until well blended. Combine buttermilk with baking soda and fold into mixture. Stir in cornmeal, flour and salt until well blended but lumpy. Do not over mix. Grease heart shaped muffin tray. Pour batter into the tray ¾ full and spoon the sautéed sugar corn over the tops. Bake in preheated oven 18-20 minutes, or until a toothpick inserted in the center comes out clean.

Sparkling Limeade ⚜

24 oz. of Sprite™
8 oz. frozen limeade concentrate
2 c. lime sherbet

2 c. crushed ice
1 fresh lime

Begin by combining half of the Sprite™, limeade, sherbet and ice in blender, mix well, add fresh lime juice and remaining sprite for desired consistency.

❧ Notes & Comments ❧

Gatherings ⚜

Week One
Evening Two

Almond Tuna Cheddar Melt

Classic flavors of flaky albacore tuna and finely minced sweet
almonds melted together with the aged goodness of sharp
cheddar cheese between buttery toasted French bread

Asiago Potato Soup

Oven roasted baby reds, smokey-sweet applewood bacon and minced
green onion in a rich and creamy Asiago cheese soup topped with
homemade croutons and fresh cilantro leaves

Strawberry Spinach Salad

Succulent fresh ripened strawberries, sweet red onion, plump yellow
raisins and crisp English cucumber tossed with garden fresh baby
spinach leaves in a savory honey Dijon dressing

Cheese Crusted Croutons

Crusty French bread toasted crisp with a rich Asiago cheese
butter, cut into bite sized crunchy croutons

Oven Roasted Sweet Potato Fries

Hearty oven roasted sweet potato slices seasoned with gently minced
fresh basil, ground black peppercorn and salt

Almond Tuna Cheddar Melt ⚜

2 cans tuna (12 oz. ea.)

2 c. almonds

½ c. green onions, minced

4-6 tbsp. mayonnaise

½ tsp. lemon juice

2 tsp. yellow mustard

1 tsp. Worcestershire sauce

1 c. sharp cheddar cheese

12 slices of French bread

3-4 tbsp. creamy butter

salt and pepper to taste

Chop almonds to a very fine consistency. Combine drained tuna, mustard, 4 tbsp. mayonnaise, lemon juice and Worcestershire sauce. Fold in almonds, minced onions and salt and pepper to taste. Mixture should be fairly dry. If a moister consistency is desired add more mayonnaise. Spread tuna mix on French bread slices (or any dense loaf) buttering each side of sandwich. In a skillet lightly grill each side. As each side is fully toasted sprinkle with sharp cheddar cheese, as it cooks turn once on each side. Serve immediately.

Asiago Potato Soup

1 lb. smoked bacon

1 tsp. onion salt

2 tsp. dried parsley flakes

1 c. butter

1–1½ c. flour

3 tsp. granulated chicken bouillon

1 tsp coarse black pepper

1 tsp. kosher salt

1 qt. half and half

1–2 qt. 2% milk

8 oz. freshly grated Asiago cheese

18 baby red potatoes

8 green onion stalks, finely chopped

¼ c. cilantro, minced

Preheat oven to 425°. Dice bacon and sauté. Remove bacon from pan and set aside. Dice baby red potatoes, with skins, into bite size pieces and toss in remaining bacon drippings to coat evenly. Spread on a baking sheet and sprinkle with parsley flakes and kosher salt. Place in oven and bake for 20–30 minutes, turning potatoes every 10 minutes until golden brown. Do not over cook. Potatoes will fry as they bake in the oven. Melt butter in a large pot with chicken bouillon, onion salt and pepper. Slowly add flour beginning with 1 c. until the butter is completely absorbed. Add more flour until mixture is crumbly. Using a whisk, slowly stir in the half and half until it is smooth. Soup will thicken as it cooks. Fold in cheese and green onions. Add fried potatoes and bacon to the soup. The consistency should be very thick. Begin slowly stirring in milk until you reach desired thickness. Top with homemade croutons, fresh cilantro and serve.

Honey Mustard Dressing ⚜

5 tbsp. extra virgin olive oil

2 tbsp. aged balsamic vinegar

1 tsp, Dijon mustard

2 tbsp. mayonnaise

2 tbsp. honey

½ tsp. salt

½ tsp. fresh ground pepper

Combine ingredients in blender and mix well. Chill before serving.

Strawberry Spinach Salad ⚜

1 lg. English cucumber

½ med. sweet red onion

15 ripened strawberries

1 c. plump yellow raisins

1 bag of spinach (20 oz.)

Rinse spinach leaves, pat dry. Dice cucumber, slice ripened strawberries, cut sweet red onion into fourths and thinly slice. Toss with fresh spinach and plump raisins. Chill, toss with dressing just before serving.

Cheese Crusted Croutons ⚜

4 slices French bread
¼ c. mayonnaise
¼ c. creamy butter
¼ c. cheddar cheese
¼ c. Asiago or Parmesan cheese
2 tsp. onion salt
coarse black pepper to taste

Turn oven temperature to broil. Mix ingredients in small bowl and spread over slices of bread. Broil in oven until golden, 2-3 minutes. Turn over and spread cheese mixture on the other side of the bread and broil again for 2-3 minutes. Let cool and slice toasted bread into cubes, serve with soup or salad.

Oven Roasted Sweet Potato Fries ⚜

4 lg. sweet potatoes
2 tbsp. extra virgin olive oil
1 tsp. ground black peppercorn
1 tsp. salt
1 tsp. fresh basil, gently minced

Preheat oven to 425°. Slice sweet potatoes into thin strips and lay them out on a baking tray. Brush with olive oil, sprinkle with fresh basil, salt and pepper. Turn over and repeat. Bake in oven for 10-12 minutes, turning twice.

Gatherings

Week One
Evening Three

Spicy Honey Glazed Chicken

Tender chicken lightly sautéed until golden, topped with a silky sweet honey glaze of smoked bacon, aged red wine vinegar and a hint of spicy Dijon mustard, served over garden fresh rice

Garden Fresh Rice

Fresh white rice tossed with fragrant gently minced dill and crisp green onion tops

Parmesan Baked Veggies

Slivered baby carrots, slender garden green beans and crisp zucchini medallions gently roasted with rich Parmesan cheese

Nine Layer Salad

A stunning display of garden goodness! Layers of crisp romaine lettuce, sweet garden peas, young crunchy celery, fragrant red onion and ripe cheddar cheese crowned with a creamy dressing, finished with crisp applewood bacon

Savory Cheddar Biscuits

Cheesy hot biscuits with a satisfying hint of garlic and thyme

Spicy Honey Glazed Chicken ⚜

4 whole chicken breasts
    boneless, skinless

1-2 tbsp. extra virgin olive oil

1 lb. smoked bacon

½ med. sweet red onion

2 c water

½ c. honey

½ c. aged red wine vinegar

2 tbsp. Dijon mustard

1½ tbsp. cornstarch

1 tsp. Tabasco™ sauce

Sauté diced bacon until crisp. Remove bacon from pan and set aside for Nine Layer Salad (pg. 27). Sauté ½ sweet red onion in remaining bacon drippings until onions are clear. Using a wire whisk, add to onion cornstarch, mustard, Tabasco™ sauce, vinegar, honey and water. Bring to a boil and simmer until sauce thickens. Set aside. Cut fresh chicken breasts into thin strips place in separate skillet and sauté in olive oil, turning occasionally until lightly golden. Place chicken strips along side rice and vegetables. Finish with warm spicy honey glaze and serve.

Garden Fresh Rice ⚜

4 c. water

1 tbsp. creamy butter

1 tsp. granulated chicken bouillon

2 c. rice

4 green onions

2 tbsp. fresh dill, gently minced

Bring water, butter and chicken bouillon to a boil. Add rice and cover with lid. Cook for 15 minutes or until holes form on top of rice. Chop green onions and mince fresh dill. Just before serving fold in fresh green onions and gently minced dill. Serve immediately.

Parmesan Baked Veggies ⚜

12 oz. baby carrots, slivered

2 skinny zucchini, sliced

12 oz. gourmet skinny green beans

¼ c. extra virgin olive oil

¾ c. Parmesan cheese, grated

½ tsp. ground black peppercorns

½ tsp. sea salt

Preheat oven to 425°. Rinse and sliver baby carrots. Clean and cut zucchini into medallions. In a Ziploc® bag combine slivered carrots, rinsed green beans and zucchini with olive oil and Parmesan cheese. Spread coated vegetables on a cookie sheet and bake for 10 minutes. Salt and pepper to taste.

Savory Cheddar Biscuits ⚜

3 c. flour

2 tbsp. sugar

¾ tsp. cream of tartar

¼ c. cream

¼ c. shortening

½ c. creamy butter

1½ c. cheddar cheese, shredded

1 tbsp. + 1 tsp. baking powder

1 tsp. salt

1 tbsp. dried minced onion

½ tsp. garlic powder

½ tsp. dried thyme

1 c. 2% milk

Preheat oven to 450°. In a large bowl stir in flour, baking powder, sugar, salt, cream of tartar, minced onion, garlic powder and thyme. Cut in the butter and shortening using a pastry blender. Cut together until mixture resembles coarse crumbs. Form a well in the center of the flour mixture. Pour in milk and cream all at once. Use a fork, stir until just moistened, fold in cheese. Be careful not to over-mix. Drop dough by spoonfuls (or use an ice cream scoop) onto a well-greased pan. Bake medium size biscuits for 10 minutes, or large biscuits for 12 minutes. Cook until slightly browned.

Nine Layer Salad

2 heads hearts of romaine lettuce
6 stalks of young celery
1 garden green pepper
1 med. sweet red onion
1 c. mayonnaise
10 oz. frozen peas
3 tbsp. sugar
1 pt. sour cream
1 lb. smoked bacon
8 oz. cheddar cheese

In a glass bowl layer lettuce, diced red onion, peas, grated cheese, chopped celery and green peppers. Blend sour cream and mayonnaise, spread like icing over top layer of salad and cover completely. Sprinkle with sugar, top with chopped bacon bits. Chill and serve.

Gatherings ⚜
Week One
Evening Four

Tri Tip Steak

Thinly sliced tender tri tip steak marinated in a sweet and spicy
pineapple teriyaki glaze, baked to perfection

Stuffed Zucchini

Slim summer garden zucchini heartily filled with spicy rich sausage and
white rice, simmered in an aromatic blend of sweet Italian tomatoes,
bay leaves and garden fresh basil until firm and tender

German Fries

Buttery Yukon potato medallions generously seasoned with
garden good green chives and hot red chilies, sautéed to
a delicious golden brown

Crunchy Cucumber Salad

Crunchy English cucumber and ripe radish slices tossed in a fresh
creamy dressing of cool yogurt and sour cream with minced dill herb,
freshly squeezed lime juice and chilled green capers

Gorgonzola Cheese Spread

Aged Gorgonzola cheese blended with tangy Worcestershire, creamy
mayonnaise, diced green chives and crushed coarse black peppercorns
served with crisp crackers or flat bread

Tri Tip Steak ⚜

3-4 lbs. tri tip steak

Place Tri Tip Steak in an air tight container with teriyaki marinade to marinate overnight or preferably 2 days. Preheat oven to 425°. Bake for 25-30 minutes for medium rare (as pictured). Remove from oven and cover with foil. Thinly slice just before serving.

Teriyaki Marinade ⚜

1 head of garlic	¼ c. teriyaki sauce	3 tbsp. fresh lemon juice
1 tbsp. extra virgin olive oil	1 tbsp. soy sauce	½ med. white onion
⅔ c. water	1 c. dark brown sugar	¼ tsp. cayenne pepper
1 c. pineapple juice	½ c. Karo™ syrup	¼ tsp. red chilies

Preheat oven to 325°. Take garlic head, cut top and bottom off so the whole garlic will sit flat, making sure the cloves stay together. Put garlic into a small oven dish, drizzle olive oil over it and cover with aluminum foil. Bake for 1 hour. Let cool.

Combine water, pineapple juice, teriyaki sauce, soy sauce and brown sugar in a saucepan over medium heat. Stir occasionally until mixture boils, reduce heat to medium low. Squeeze heads of garlic to remove garlic paste. Discard garlic skin, combine paste and remaining ingredients. Continue to simmer for 25 minutes. Marinade will be thick and syrupy. Make sure it does not boil over. Stir occasionally. *Helpful Hint: Makes a great teriyaki marinade for chicken or a flavorful glaze over rice.*

Stuffed Zucchini ⚜

8 fresh slim zucchini	1 tsp. fresh ground black peppercorn
1 c. water	2 fresh bay leaves
3 tbsp. sugar	1 tbsp. aged balsamic vinegar
2 tbsp. creamy butter	2 tbsp. fresh basil, gently minced
1½ c. Minute Rice™	2 cans Italian recipe stewed tomatoes (14.5 oz. ea.)
2 tsp. sea salt	1 lb. spicy ground sausage

Cut off ends of rinsed zucchini. Cut in 3-4" lengths and core center completely. In a bowl, mix sausage with rice, 1 tsp. salt and ½ tsp. pepper, balsamic vinegar and fresh minced basil. Stuff cut zucchini pieces with sausage and rice mixture. If any sausage mix is left over form small meat balls. In a deep frying pan, melt butter, add cans of Italian stewed tomatoes and bay leaves. Sprinkle with sugar, 1 tsp. salt and ½ tsp. pepper. Simmer for 6-8 minutes. Add the stuffed zucchini to the stewed tomatoes. Pour water in pan making sure not to completely cover with water. Cover pan with lid. Simmer on low for 20 minutes. Be careful not to over cook. The zucchini should remain firm.

German Fries ⚜

10 Yukon potatoes
2 tsp. extra virgin olive oil
1 tbsp. dried chives
1/8 tsp. red chilies
1 tsp. kosher salt
1/2 tsp. coarse black peppercorns

Preheat oven to 400°. Bake medium size potatoes for 30 minutes. Mix dry ingredients together to create a seasoning mix. Cut potatoes into medallion slices, drizzle 1-2 tsp. of olive oil in frying pan. Sauté potato medallions, generously seasoning with mix. Turn over and season again, cooking until crisp and golden. Serve immediately.

Gorgonzola Cheese Spread ⚜

8 oz. aged Gorgonzola cheese, crumbled
1/3 c. mayonnaise
1/2 tsp. Worcestershire sauce
1 tsp. dried chives
1/8 tsp. coarse pepper

Combine all ingredients in bowl and microwave for 1-1 1/2 minutes. Spread on any desired thin cracker or flat bread.

Crunchy Cucumber Salad ⚜

4 English cucumbers
24 radishes
½ c. capers
¼ c. plain yogurt
⅓ c. sour cream

2 tbsp. fresh dill, gently minced
2 tbsp. freshly squeezed lime juice
½ tsp. savory garlic salt
½ tsp. kosher salt
1 tsp. fresh ground black peppercorn

Thinly slice radishes and chop cucumbers. Place in bowl and set aside. In small bowl combine yogurt, sour cream, lime juice, minced dill, garlic salt, salt and pepper. Pour dressing over cucumbers and radishes, fold in capers and chill.

⚜ *Shopping List* ⚜

each recipe is designed to serve six

chicken breasts, 8 whole boneless, skinless
cooked bay shrimp, 2 lbs.
smoked bacon, 3 lbs.
ground spicy sausage, 1 lb.
tuna, 2 cans (12 oz. ea.)
French bread, 16 slices
cilantro, ¾ c.
fresh bay leaves, 2
fresh dill, ¾ c.
fresh basil, 3 tbsp.
garlic, 1 head
fresh slim zucchini, 10
avocado, 2 medium
cabbage, 2 c. shredded
cauliflower, 1 head
red onion, 2 medium
green onions, 28
white onion, 1 medium
red bell pepper, 1 medium
yellow bell pepper, 1 medium
green bell pepper, 1 medium
tomato, 1 large

thin green beans, 4 c.
spinach, 1 bag (20 oz.)
English cucumber, 5
baby carrots, 12 oz.
lime, 4
lemon, 3
radishes, 24
Yukon potatoes, 10
baby red potatoes, 18 small
strawberries, 15 ripened
corn on the cob, 1 ear
sweet potatoes, 4 large
hearts of romaine lettuce, 2 heads
celery, 6 stalks
sharp cheddar cheese, 3 ⅓ c.
Gorgonzola cheese, 8 oz. aged
Asiago cheese, 8 oz. fresh grated
Parmesan cheese, ¾ c.
plain yogurt, ¼ c.
sour cream, 2 ⅓ c.
buttermilk, 1 c.
half and half, 4 c.

cream, 1/4 c.

plump yellow raisins, 1 c.

Dijon mustard , 3 tbsp.

cream of tartar, 3/4 tsp.

cornmeal, 1 c.

cornstarch, 1 1/2 tbsp.

almonds, 2 c.

rice, 5 c.

Minute Rice™, 1 1/2 c.

pineapple juice, 1 c.

teriyaki sauce, 1/4 c.

capers, 1/2 c.

Tabasco™ sauce, 1 tsp.

salsa, 1 c.

Italian stewed tomatoes, 2 cans (14.5 oz. ea.)

frozen peas, 10 oz.

frozen limeade concentrate, 8 oz.

crushed ice, 2 c.

lime sherbet, 2 c.

Sprite™, 24 oz.

tortilla chips, 1 c.

corn tortillas, 18 small fresh

Ranch Dressing Mix or see Homemade Dry
Ranch Mix (pg. 188)

⚜ *Staples* ⚜

flour	dried chives	honey
milk	cayenne pepper	baking powder
eggs	cumin	baking soda
creamy butter	dried parsley flakes	shortening
sugar	red chilies	granulated chicken bullion
dark brown sugar	dried minced onion	soy sauce
sea salt	garlic powder	classic yellow mustard
coarse black pepper	dried thyme	Worcestershire sauce
onion salt	mayonnaise	extra virgin olive oil
savory garlic salt	Karo™ syrup	aged balsamic vinegar

CHAPTER TWO

Gatherings

Week Two
Evening One

Chicken Cordon Bleu

Thinly sliced tender chicken breasts layered with aged Swiss cheese,
delicate ham slices rolled and finished with a creamy cheese white
wine sauce and an herbed toasted topping

Butternut Squash

Garden fresh butternut squash baked to sweet perfection tossed with
brown sugar, flavorful minced ginger, creamy butter and
a dash of aromatic anise seed

Honey Glazed Walnut Rolls

Oven fresh home baked rolls topped with a buttery sweet honey glaze
of ground cinnamon and crunchy chopped walnuts

Asparagus Wild Rice

A satisfying blend of nutty wild and fluffy white rice, fresh
tender green asparagus tips and sweet creamy butter

Beet Salad

Sweet pickled beets, crunchy hearts of romaine lettuce and aged
Parmesan cheese tossed in a chilled Honey Dijon Vinaigrette
with just a hint of fresh garlic topped with
freshly ground black peppercorns

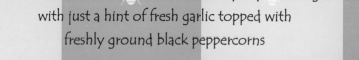

Chicken Cordon Bleu ⚜

3 whole chicken breasts
        boneless, skinless
1 lb. thinly sliced ham
16 oz. Swiss cheese
8 oz. cream cheese, softened
2 ½ c. hot water
3 tsp. granulated chicken bouillon
½ c. white cooking wine
½ tsp. salt
½ tsp. pepper
½ c. butter
3 c. seasoned dry bread crumbs
toothpicks

Preheat oven to 350°. Slice each chicken breast in half, cutting down the middle. Divide each half cutting across from side to side into three very thin slices. Between two sheets of wax paper, tenderize the pieces on both sides using a meat mallet. Cut the Swiss cheese into ½" x 2" cubes. Lay the chicken flat, place a slice of ham on the chicken and a cheese cube. Roll up chicken with ham and cheese, pierce with a toothpick through the middle to hold its shape. Place each chicken roll side by side in a 9" x 13" pan. If there is excess cheese, cut into cubes and place in the pan between the rolls of chicken. Sprinkle salt and pepper over the chicken. In blender combine cream cheese, water, bouillon and cooking wine, purée. Pour the sauce over the chicken rolls. Toss bread crumbs in melted butter and spread over chicken and sauce. Cover with aluminum foil. Bake for 45-55 minutes. Makes 18 Chicken Cordon Bleu rolls.

Butternut Squash ⚜

1 sweet garden butternut squash

½ tsp. anise seed

1 tbsp. freshly minced ginger

4 tbsp. brown sugar

5 tbsp. melted butter

Preheat oven to 350°. Peel squash and cut into 1″ pieces. Place in a buttered dish. Melt butter in microwave and add spices and brown sugar. Pour over squash and cover. Bake for 30 minutes. Salt and pepper to taste.

Asparagus Wild Rice ⚜

2 c. white rice

2 tsp. granulated chicken bouillon

2 c. wild rice

1 lg. bundle of asparagus

4 tbsp. creamy butter

In two separate pots place white and wild rice substituting chicken bouillon for salt and add 2 tbsp. butter to each pot and continue preparing rice according to instructions. Take clean asparagus and bend near the bottom to find natural break, snap end off, discard tough pieces and chop remaining asparagus pieces. When the white rice is cooked, turn off heat, add asparagus pieces and cover with lid. When wild rice is completely cooked fold into white rice and asparagus, toss together and serve.

Honey Glazed Walnut Rolls ⚜

2/3 c. nonfat dry milk	1/3 c. sugar	2 pkg. dry yeast (2 tbsp.)	1 egg
2 c. warm water	1/3 c. butter	5-6 c. flour	2 1/2 tsp. salt

In a bowl using an electric mixer, combine yeast and water. Let stand 5 minutes. Add sugar, butter, salt, dry milk, 2 c. flour and egg. Beat together until smooth. Add 3 1/2 c. of flour, one cup at a time and beat until smooth. Turn dough onto a lightly floured surface and knead until smooth. Brush dough with butter and return to bowl. Let rise in a warm place until it triples in size. Dust surface with flour for rolling and shaping dough. Cut or mold into desired shapes. Place on greased baking sheets. Brush surface of rolls with melted butter. Let rise in warm place for 1 1/2 hours. Preheat oven to 400°. Bake rolls for 10 minutes, remove from oven, cover with Honey Walnut Glaze. Return rolls to oven and bake for an additional 10 minutes or until golden brown.

Honey Walnut Glaze ⚜

1/2 c. liquid honey
1/3 c. granulated sugar
1/4 c. finely chopped walnuts
3 tbsp. creamy butter
1/8 tsp. ground cinnamon

Mix ingredients together and heat. Do not boil. Remove from heat and slightly cool. Bake rolls for 10 minutes. Take out of oven and spoon on Honey Walnut Glaze. Return to oven and bake rolls for an additional 10 minutes or until golden brown.

Beet Salad ⚜

2 heads hearts of romaine lettuce
2 c. sweet pickled beets

6 oz. block of Parmesan cheese
½ tsp. freshly ground black peppercorn

Clean and tear lettuce. Chill. Slice beets into small pieces. Using a cheese slicer cut Parmesan cheese into flat pieces. Add cheese and beets to chilled lettuce, top with coarse ground pepper and Honey Dijon Vinaigrette.

Honey Dijon Vinaigrette ⚜

2 tbsp. Dijon mustard
1 sm. garlic clove
6 tbsp. white wine vinegar
½ c. extra virgin olive oil
2 tbsp. mayonnaise

4 tbsp. honey
2 tbsp. sugar
¼ tsp. salt
½ tsp. pepper
1 tsp. capers

Place all ingredients in food processor and slowly add oil, blend until mixture emulsifies. Toss lightly with salad.

Gatherings
Week Two
Evening Two

Gorgonzola Crusted Beef Tenderloin

Juicy seared beef tenderloin medallions crusted with a
flavorful mixture of ripe Gorgonzola cheese crumbles, seasoned bread
crumbs and minced garden fresh parsley, basil and chives

White Wine Brussels Sprouts

Fresh small brussels sprout halves sautéed until golden brown in sweet
creamy butter and steamed to tenderness in a white
wine and savory chicken broth glaze

Glazed Long Grain Rice

Steamed long grain white rice finished with a savory chicken broth and
white wine glaze, topped with tender green onion stalks

Whole Wheat Mini Loaves

Hearty oven baked, whole wheat mini loaves sprinkled with
coarse kosher salt and served with sweet creamy butter

Strawberry Greens

Crisp garden fresh red lettuce leaves, sliced sweet summer
strawberries, toasted slivered almonds and plump dried cherries tossed
in a delicious aged Red Wine Peppercorn Dressing

Gorgonzola Crusted Beef Tenderloin ⚜

6 beef tenderloin medallions (6 oz. ea.)

1 tsp. salt

1 tsp. ground black peppercorn

1 tbsp. extra virgin olive oil

1 c. seasoned dry bread crumbs

1 c. Gorgonzola cheese

¼ c. fresh parsley, minced

¼ c. fresh chives, finely minced

⅓ c. fresh basil, gently minced

¼ tsp. salt and pepper

Preheat oven to 425°. Season medallions with kosher salt and pepper. In a pan, sear on high heat the medallions in oil. Using tongs sear all edges and sides. Place medallions on cookie sheet, set aside. Combine bread crumbs, cheese, parsley, chives, basil and ¼ tsp. salt and pepper. Mix thoroughly, pack bread crumb mixture on top and sides of each medallion. Bake in the oven for 20-25 minutes. Serve immediately.

White Wine Brussels Sprouts ⚜

24 sm. brussels sprouts
2 tbsp. creamy butter
1 c. savory chicken broth
1 c. aged white cooking wine

Rinse brussels sprouts, cut off ends and slice in half. In a large skillet sauté butter and brussels sprouts face down for 2-3 minutes, until golden. Quickly pour in chicken broth and white wine, cover with lid and steam for 3 minutes. Set aside juices to use as glaze over the rice.

Glazed Long Grain Rice ⚜

3 c. rice
6 c. water
2 tbsp. butter
2 green onions
1½ tsp. granulated chicken bouillon
fresh ground pepper to taste

Add chicken bouillon and butter to water, bring to a boil. Fold in rice and cover tightly, do not stir. Cook for 15-20 minutes or until the top of the rice is covered with tiny holes. Stir in the juice glaze from the brussels sprouts. Top with diced green onions and pepper to taste.

Whole Wheat Mini Loaves ⚜

1 tbsp. dry yeast

3 tbsp. brown sugar

1 c. warm water

2 1/4 c. whole wheat flour

1 tsp. kosher salt

1 tbsp. canola oil

1 egg white

Place yeast, sugar and water in a large bowl and allow mixture to become bubbly. In separate bowl mix together 2 c. whole wheat flour and salt. Blend with liquid mixture. Knead by hand for about 10 minutes or until smooth and elastic; add additional flour if necessary. Cut dough into four balls and roll them into 6" loaves and place 2" apart on cookie sheet. Drizzle canola oil over the tops of loaves and with a pastry brush coat evenly. Take a knife and slice diagonal cuts along the top of each loaf. Cover with a towel and let rise 1 hour, or until doubled in size. Preheat oven to 450°. Using a pastry brush cover tops of each loaf with egg white and sprinkle with kosher salt. Bake for 20-25 minutes.

Strawberry Greens ⚜

2 heads red leaf lettuce

3 c. sweet sliced strawberries

1½ c. plump dried cherries

¾ c. toasted slivered almonds

Preheat oven to 375°. On a cookie sheet, spread slivered almonds and bake for 10-12 minutes, until golden brown. Wash and rinse red leaf lettuce, tear into small pieces. Chill. Slice strawberries, toss with lettuce, almonds and plump dried cherries. Top with Red Wine Peppercorn Dressing and serve.

Red Wine Peppercorn Dressing ⚜

½ c. aged red wine vinegar

½ c. sugar

½ c. vegetable oil

½ tsp. fresh ground black peppercorn

½ tsp. sea salt

¼ tsp. Tabasco™ sauce

Blend together and chill.

Gatherings ⚜
Week Two
Evening Three

Chicken Pita Sandwiches

Shredded tender white chicken, succulent red grapes and toasted
slivered almonds married in a rich and creamy dressing served with
crunchy romaine lettuce in a warm fresh pita

Bacon Bow Tie Salad

Crisp smoky bacon pieces, gently minced purple cabbage, crisp sugar
snap peas and tender bow tie pasta, chilled and tossed in
a creamy fresh Dill Dressing

Dill Dressing

Gently minced fresh dill, cool sour cream, freshly squeezed
lime juice with a hint of sugar and a dusting of salt and
fresh ground pepper

Artichoke Delight

Steamed garden fresh artichoke generously topped with a warm,
mellow Parmesan cheese spread and oven roasted to perfection

Chicken Pita Sandwiches

2 cans of white chicken (12.5 oz. ea.)

1 head hearts of romaine lettuce

¾ c. toasted slivered almonds

3 c. sweet red seedless grapes

⅓ c. mayonnaise

2 tbsp. sugar

3 tbsp. classic yellow mustard

2 tsp. Worcestershire sauce

1 tsp. kosher salt

½ tsp. coarse ground pepper

6 pita pocket breads

Preheat oven to 375°. Place slivered almonds on cookie sheet and bake for 10 minutes or until golden brown. Drain canned chicken. Wash and clean hearts of romaine lettuce and tear into bite size pieces. In a bowl combine mayonnaise, mustard, sugar, salt, pepper and Worcestershire sauce. Whisk together. Fold in chicken with a fork creating a tuna-like consistency. Add toasted almonds and grapes. Chill before serving. When ready to serve, slice pitas in half and line bottom of pocket with lettuce. Stuff with chicken salad and serve.

Bacon Bow Tie Salad ⚜

1 lb. bag of bow tie pasta	2 c. sugar snap peas
2 lbs. smoked bacon	½ c. purple cabbage, minced

Cook pasta in salty water following instructions on the bag. Sauté bacon and break into 1" pieces (same size as the bow tie pasta). Mince purple cabbage. Clean and cut sugar snap peas in half. Toss together. Add dressing just before serving. Pepper to taste.

Dill Dressing ⚜

2 tbsp. fresh dill, gently minced	2 tbsp. sour cream	½ tsp. salt
2/3 c. mayonnaise	3 tbsp. freshly squeezed lime juice	½ tsp. fresh ground pepper
3 tbsp. sugar		

Whisk all ingredients together and chill.

Artichoke Delight ⚜

3 lg. artichokes
⅓ c. creamy butter
⅓ c. mayonnaise

⅔ c. freshly grated Parmesan cheese
⅛ tsp. coarse ground pepper
½ tsp kosher salt

Blend together softened butter, mayonnaise, cheese, salt and pepper to make a cheese spread. Cut off stems of artichokes. In a large pot steam 3 artichokes in 1 quart of water and 2 tsp. kosher salt for 45 minutes with the lid on. Cook until tender. Remove from pot and cut down the middle of each artichoke. Using cheese mixture generously spread over the flat side of the artichoke. Broil in oven for 10 minutes on the bottom shelf. Serve immediately.

Notes & Comments

Gatherings ⚜
Week Two
Evening Four

Favorite Meat Ball Spaghetti

Al dente spaghetti noodles topped with fresh garlic, basil and herb cream cheese Tuscan Sauce, spicy pork and beef meatballs with savory Italian seasonings, finished with garden fresh basil

Tuscan Marinara Sauce

A savory blend of sweetened garden tomatoes, sautéed with fresh herbs and creamy cheese to create a classic favorite

Fresh Mozzarella Salad

Delicate mozzarella balls rolled in fresh basil and pine nut pesto for a flavorful addition to a salad of romaine lettuce, ripe cherry tomatoes and plump black olives, chilled and drizzled with Aged Balsamic Vinaigrette

Aged Balsamic Vinaigrette

A light blend of aged balsamic vinegar, extra virgin olive oil, sweet honey, spicy Dijon mustard and savory seasonings

Focaccia Bread

Robust oven baked Italian bread crust brushed with sweet creamy butter and served with herb infused olive oil for dipping

Favorite Meat Ball Spaghetti ⚜

1½ lbs. ground beef	1 tsp. thyme	2 eggs
½ lb. spicy ground pork	1 tsp. Italian seasonings	½ c. water
1 ½ tsp. dried oregano	2 tbsp. fresh minced parsley	¾ c. seasoned dry bread crumbs
2 tsp. fresh basil, minced	½ tsp. pepper	1 ½ tbsp. Worcestershire sauce
1 tsp. garlic powder	2 tsp. kosher salt	

Fold together all ingredients and form 8 large meat balls. In large, deep skillet sauté meat balls in 2 tbsp. olive oil and salt. Continue turning meat balls until they are browned on all sides.

Tuscan Marinara Sauce ⚜

1 can tomato sauce (29 oz.)	2 tsp. dried oregano	2 tsp. extra virgin olive oil
1 can crushed tomatoes (28 oz.)	¼ c. fresh basil, chopped	1½ tsp. salt
1½ tsp. fresh garlic, minced	½ c. sugar	1 tsp. fresh ground black pepper
1 med. onion, diced	2 tsp. dried thyme	6 oz. cream cheese

Remove browned meatballs from skillet. Using drippings add 2 tbsp. olive oil and sauté minced garlic and onion on high for 2-3 minutes. Stir in salt and pepper, oregano, thyme and fresh basil. Continue to sauté until onions are clear. Fold in tomato sauce, crushed tomatoes, sugar and cream cheese, add 1 c. water and stir well. Place meatballs in sauce and cover with a lid. Simmer for ½ an hour making sure to cook large meat balls thoroughly. Cook spaghetti noodles al dente and place noodles on each plate. Add one large meatball to the middle of each plate, top with sauce and finish with fresh chopped basil.

Mozzarella Salad ⚜

2 heads hearts of romaine lettuce

2 c. ripe cherry tomatoes

2 c. plump black olives

2 c. mozzarella balls, rolled in fresh pesto

Clean and tear lettuce, toss with tomatoes, olives and mozzarella balls. Chill, drizzle with Aged Balsamic Vinaigrette Dressing and serve.

Fresh Pesto ⚜

¾ c. fresh basil, diced

⅓ c. fresh parsley, chopped

⅓ c. fresh Parmesan cheese, grated

1 clove garlic, minced

2½ tbsp. extra virgin olive oil

1½ tbsp. soft salted butter

1 tbsp. pine nuts

¼ tsp. salt and fresh ground pepper

Purée all ingredients together in food processor. Take ready-made mozzarella balls and roll in fresh pesto sauce. Refrigerate and set aside. Serve with salad.

1½ lb. sm. fresh mozzarella balls

Aged Balsamic Vinaigrette ⚜

⅓ c. extra virgin olive oil

¼ c. aged balsamic vinegar

2 tsp. honey

1 tsp. spicy Dijon mustard

2 green onion stalks, minced

¼ tsp. sea salt

¼ tsp. coarse pepper

Mix together well and chill. Shake vigorously before serving.

Focaccia Bread ⚜

1 tbsp. dry yeast	1 c. warm water	2 ½ c. white flour
1 tbsp. canola oil	2 tbsp. creamy butter	1 tsp. kosher salt
1 tbsp. sugar		

Place yeast, sugar and water in a large bowl or food processor and allow the mixture to become bubbly. Mix in 2 c. of flour and salt. Knead for about 10 minutes or mix in food processor for 15 seconds, until smooth and elastic. Add more flour if necessary. Brush the sides of a bowl with oil, place dough in bowl and cover. Let dough rise in a warm place for 1 hour, until doubled in size.

Punch down dough and divide in half. Let the dough rest for a few minutes. Coat two 9"x9" pans with nonstick spray. Press dough into pans. Melt butter and brush over the tops of loaves. Let dough rise again until doubled, about 45 minutes.

Preheat oven to 450°. Lightly sprinkle salt over the loaves. Bake for 20-25 minutes, until lightly browned.

Notes & Comments

⚜ *Shopping List* ⚜

each recipe is designed to serve six

chicken breasts, 3 whole boneless, skinless

chicken, 2 cans of white (12.5 oz. ea.)

ham, 1 lb. thinly sliced

smoked bacon, 2 lbs.

ground beef, 1½ lbs.

spicy ground pork, ½ lb.

beef tenderloin medallions, 6 (6 oz. ea.)

purple cabbage, ½ c.

hearts of romaine lettuce, 5 heads

ripe cherry tomatoes, 2 c.

red leaf lettuce, 2 heads

brussels sprouts, 24 small

sweet garden squash, 1 large

artichokes, 3 large

Asparagus, 1 large bundle

sugar snap peas, 2 c.

green onions, 4

onions, 2 medium

fresh ginger, 1 tbsp.

fresh basil, 1½ c.

fresh parsley, ⅔ c.

fresh garlic, 1½ tbsp.

fresh chives, ¼ c.

fresh dill, 2 tbsp.

strawberries, 3 c. sweet sliced

grapes, 3 c. sweet red seedless

lime, 3

Swiss cheese, 16 oz.

cream cheese, 20 oz.

fresh mozzarella, 1 lb. small balls

Parmesan cheese, 6 oz. block

Parmesan cheese, ⅔ c., freshly grated

Gorgonzola cheese, 1 c.

sour cream, 2 tbsp.

white cooking wine, 1½ c.

white wine vinegar, 6 tbsp.

red wine vinegar, ¼ c.

chicken broth, 1 c.

black olives, 2 c.

sweet pickled beets, 2 c.

capers, 1 tsp.

tomato sauce, 2 cans (29 oz. ea.)

crushed tomatoes, 2 cans (28 oz.)
Tabasco™ sauce, ¼ tsp.
spicy Dijon mustard, 1 tsp.
white rice, 5 c.
wild rice, 2 c.
nonfat dry milk, ⅔ c.
whole wheat flour, 2¼ c.
dry yeast, 3 pkg.

walnuts, ¼ c.
almonds, 1½ c. slivered
pine nuts, 1 tbsp.
plump dried cherries, 1½ c.
bow tie pasta, 1 lb. bag
pita breads, 6 pockets
seasoned dry bread crumbs, 4¾ c.
toothpicks

⚜ *Staples* ⚜

flour
eggs
butter
sugar
brown sugar
kosher salt
fresh ground black pepper
Italian seasonings

dried oregano
thyme, dried
oregano, dried
garlic powder
anise seed
cinnamon, ground
granulated chicken bullion.
balsamic vinegar

extra virgin olive oil
vegetable oil
canola oil
honey
classic yellow mustard
mayonnaise
Worcestershire sauce

CHAPTER THREE

Gatherings ⚜

Week Three
Evening One

Harvest Chicken & Yams

Festive layers of tender white chicken breast, sweet meaty yams, fresh
baby spinach and aged Swiss cheese melted together with a warm white
wine cream sauce and fresh chopped chives

Roasted Barley

Soft barley pearls pan roasted until golden brown, steamed in a savory
chicken broth and finished with fresh chopped basil and
tender green onions

Boston Brown Bread

Wheat, rye and corn flours combine for a satisfyingly dense bread
drizzled with the natural goodness of honey and served
warm from the oven with a creamy butter ball

Steamed Asparagus

Tender fresh asparagus spears steamed and neatly finished with
savory sea salt and sweet creamy butter

Crimson Grape Salad

Crisp crimson red grapes smothered in cool sour cream with earthy
oven roasted walnuts and rich sweet brown sugar

Harvest Chicken & Yams ⚜

4 tender chicken breasts, boneless, skinless

4 sweet yams

16 oz. Swiss cheese

10 oz. fresh spinach

¾ c. aged white cooking wine

½ c. cream

2 tbsp. granulated chicken bouillon

2 tbsp. chives

½ tsp. salt

1 tsp. coarse ground pepper

Preheat oven to 325°. Cut each chicken breast into three thin slices. Tenderize each piece with meat mallet between two sheets of wax paper and set aside. Cut Swiss cheese into thin slices, peel and slice yams into large round pieces. Spray 9" X 13" pan with cooking spray. Begin with a layer of yams, fit tightly together, followed by a layer of tenderized chicken pieces, cover with cheese slices and all of the spinach. Repeat yams and chicken, topped with cheese. Sprinkle with granulated chicken bouillon, salt and pepper. Pour white cooking wine and cream over entire dish. Finish with chives and coarse ground pepper, cover with aluminum foil. Bake for 50-60 minutes. Cut in squares to serve.

Roasted Barley ⚜

3 tsp. butter
2 c. pearl barley
6 c. chicken broth

½ tsp. salt
⅔ c. fresh basil, minced
½ c. green onion, diced

Heat butter in a large skillet over medium heat. Add barley and sauté for 5 minutes until browned, stirring constantly. Add chicken broth and salt, bring to a boil. Cover, reduce heat and simmer 45 minutes or until barley is tender and liquid is absorbed. Remove from heat. Stir in minced basil and diced green onions.

Boston Brown Bread ⚜

1 c. whole wheat flour
1 c. rye flour
1 c. yellow cornmeal
1½ tsp. baking soda

1½ tsp. salt
1½ c. honey
2 c. buttermilk
½ c. butter

Preheat oven to 350°. Prepare 9"x 13" pan with cooking spray. In medium mixing bowl combine flours, cornmeal, soda and salt. Stir in ¾ c. honey and buttermilk. Pour mixture into a 9"x 13" pan and cover with a moist towel, let sit for 30 minutes. Using a melon baller, prepare butter balls with room temperature butter. Place the butter balls on a plate and refrigerate until ready to serve. Bake bread mixture for 25 minutes, remove from oven, lightly poke holes in the top and spread ½ c. honey over the top. Place back in oven for an additional 10 minutes. While warm, cut in squares, drizzle with ¼ c. honey and serve with butter ball.

Steamed Asparagus ⚜

2 bundles of tender asparagus
1 tsp. sea salt
2 tbsp. creamy butter

Prepare rinsed asparagus by bending near the bottom to find natural break, snap end off, discard tough pieces. Bring 2 c. water and salt to a boil and place asparagus in water. Cover with lid and boil for 1-2 minutes. Drain asparagus, place in serving dish, top with butter and serve immediately.

Crimson Grape Salad ⚜

8 c. crimson red seedless grapes (2 c. = 1 lb.)
1½ c. sour cream
2 c. walnuts, toasted
1 c. brown sugar

Preheat oven to 350°. Toast walnuts in oven for 10-12 minutes. Let cool. Remove grapes from stems, rinse clean and dry. Fold in cool toasted walnuts and sour cream. Place salad in wide, open dish and sprinkle with brown sugar just before serving.

⚜ Notes & Comments ⚜

Gatherings

Week Three
Evening Two

Ginger Glazed Kabobs

Tender marinated flank steak strips woven onto kabob sticks,
quickly grilled and drizzled with a silky sweet honey
ginger and aged balsamic vinegar glaze

Baby Red Mashed Potatoes

Seasoned baby red potatoes whipped with sweet
creamy butter and fresh whole milk

Carrots & Sugar Snap Peas

Lightly steamed sweet garden carrots and crisp sugar snap peas
tossed with fresh basil leaves and creamy butter

Feta Cheese Toast

Fresh basil and oregano butter with ripe crumbled feta cheese
spread on oven fresh baguettes, toasted to a
warm golden brown finish

Candied Pecan Salad

Oven roasted sweetened pecans, crisp tart red apples, ripened Roma
tomatoes and freshly grated Parmesan cheese atop a bed of fresh
red leaf lettuce with Sweet Poppy Seed Dressing

Ginger Glazed Kabobs

3 lbs. flank steak

6 tbsp. fresh ginger, minced

1 c. extra virgin olive oil

3 c. honey

1½ c. white wine vinegar

¾ c. aged balsamic vinegar

1½ tsp. coarse ground black peppercorn

1½ tsp. kosher salt

Make shallow diagonal cuts on both sides of flank steak to create a tenderizing effect. Cut steak on the diagonal in long strips about ¾" thick. Mix all other ingredients together to make marinade. Take half of the marinade and pour over the flank steak pieces and let it marinate overnight or at least 2-3 hours. Weave steak pieces on kabob sticks and cook on grill for 2-3 minutes on each side. Do not over cook. Take the remaining half of the fresh marinade and simmer to a reduction for 6 -8 minutes until a thick glaze forms. Drizzle over potatoes and kabobs just before serving.

Baby Red Mashed Potatoes ⚜

4 lbs. baby red potatoes
½–1 c. milk
½ c. creamy butter

1 tsp. kosher salt
1 tsp. coarse ground black peppercorn

Clean and peel leaving half of the skin on the baby red potatoes. Boil until tender to the fork, adding 2 tsp. kosher salt to the water. Drain potatoes, place butter and ½ c. of milk in pot. Whip potatoes adding enough milk for desired consistency. Add salt and pepper. Serve on plate, top with 2 kabobs of flank steak, drizzle with ginger glaze and serve.

Carrots & Sugar Snap Peas ⚜

4 c. garden carrots
2 c. sugar snap peas
½ tsp. kosher salt
¼ c creamy butter
¼ c. fresh basil, minced
3 tbsp. sugar

Rinse and peel large carrots and cut in 1" diagonal pieces. In a pot bring 2 c. water and 3 tbsp. of sugar to a boil. Add carrots and cook for 3–4 minutes. Add snap peas and cook for 1 more minute. Drain water and toss with butter, salt and fresh basil. Serve immediately.

Feta Cheese Toast ⚜

1 baguette	1/8 tsp. oregano
5 oz. feta cheese crumbled	1/2 tsp. dried basil
3 tbsp. softened butter	1/4 tsp. sea salt
4 tbsp. mayonnaise	1/8 tsp. crushed black peppercorn

Combine crumbled feta cheese, softened butter, mayonnaise, oregano, dried basil, sea salt and crushed black peppercorn to make a cheese spread. Cut baguette into ¾" slices. Top with cheese spread and broil in oven until browned. Serve.

Candied Pecan Salad ⚜

2 heads red leaf lettuce
1 c. freshly grated Parmesan cheese
1½ c. whole pecans

¾ c. sugar
2 crisp red apples
¾ c. ripened Roma tomatoes

Clean and tear red leaf lettuce, chill. In a heavy skillet place pecans and sugar. Cook on low heat until sugar dissolves and pecans are fully coated. Stir continually once sugar begins to melt. Set aside to cool. Cut apples into thin slices. Grate cheese and add tomatoes. Toss together or arrange individually on salad plate (as pictured). Top with Sweet Poppy Seed Dressing.

Sweet Poppy Seed Dressing ⚜

½ c. sugar
¾ c. raspberry vinegar
⅓ c. vegetable oil
½ med. sweet red onion
⅛ tsp. salt
⅛ tsp. black pepper
¾ tsp. dry mustard
1 tbsp. poppy seeds

Cut onion in half. Blend all ingredients in blender except the poppy seeds. Puree dressing. Fold in poppy seeds. Chill.

Gatherings ⚜

Week Three
Evening Three

Sausage Potato Cakes

A crowd pleasing comfort food. Rich and spicy fresh
ground sausage, garlic, chive and mashed red potato patties
lightly fried until crisp and golden brown

Sweet Stuffed French Toast

Sweetened maple glazed pecans surround layers of
French toast, stuffed with whipped cream cheese and
sweetened cinnamon. Served with a dollop of fresh
whipped cream while still warm from the oven.

Fruit Medley

Fresh plump blueberries, delicately sweet summer raspberries,
succulent vine ripened blackberries and sun sweetened
pineapple chunks drizzled with a light, citrusy fruit glaze

Fruit Glaze

This unique glaze combines the tart taste of freshly squeezed lime
juice, blended with sweetened marshmallow fluff
and softened smooth cream cheese. It is the
perfect finish for this fruit medley

Sausage Potato Cakes ⚜

10 baby red potatoes

1 lb. spicy ground sausage

1 tsp. garlic pepper blend

2 tsp. dried chives

1 tsp. sea salt

2 tbsp. creamy butter

Peel and boil potatoes, drain, add butter, salt and garlic pepper blend, mashing until smooth, but firm. Sauté ground sausage, remove from pan leaving sausage drippings in skillet. Blend potatoes, sausage and chives together and form into patties. Lightly fry potato sausage patties in remaining sausage drippings until golden. Place on pan uncovered and keep warm in 275° oven until ready to serve. Patties will become crispy in the oven.

Sweet Stuffed French Toast ⚜

10 slices of bread	¼ c. maple syrup	3 eggs
3 oz. cream cheese	1 c. pecans	1 c. 1% milk
¾ c. brown sugar	3 tbsp. sugar	1 tbsp. vanilla
⅓ c. creamy butter	½ tsp. ground cinnamon	⅛ tsp. nutmeg

Preheat oven to 350°. To make sugar pecan glaze melt butter in microwave, add maple syrup, brown sugar and pecans, mix well. Spray a 9"x9" dish with cooking spray, and spread sugar pecan glaze in the bottom, saving ¼ c. to spread on top layer. In a small bowl combine 3 tbsp. sugar with ground cinnamon. Fold into whipped cream cheese. Cut crust off bread slices and spread cream cheese on 5 slices, top with remaining slices and place over sugar pecan glaze in bottom of dish. Lightly beat the eggs, milk, vanilla and nutmeg. Pour over the bread. Spread remaining sugar pecan glaze on top of bread layer and bake for 30-35 minutes or until golden brown. Let cool for at least 10 minutes before serving. Top with sour cream or whipped cream and berries (optional).

Fruit Medley ⚜

2 c. fresh blueberries

2 c. ripe raspberries

2 c. plump blackberries

2 c. pineapple tidbits

Rinse berries and drain pineapple tidbits. Toss together and drizzle with glaze.

Fruit Glaze ⚜

4 tbsp. cream cheese   juice of 2 limes   1 c. marshmallow whip

Warm cream cheese in microwave for 10-12 seconds to soften. Fold together with marshmallow whip and fresh lime juice. Chill.

❦ Notes & Comments ❦

Gatherings ⚜

Week Three
Evening Four

Sweet & Sour Chicken

Morsels of tender Asian fried chicken breast slowly simmered in a
tangy sweet and sour sauce served on a bed of delicately thin
Chinese noodles with a heaping scoop of steamed rice,
garnished with stir fried vegetables.

Stir Fried Vegetables

Garden fresh medley of julienned red and yellow bell peppers, sweet
garden carrots, fresh young onions and crisp sugar snap peas gently
stir fried in savory hot chili sesame oil

Savory Mushroom Stock

Steamy savory soul warming beef flavored broth
with tender gently minced green onions and slivers of
fresh sultry mushrooms

Sweet & Sour Chicken ⚜

8 chicken breast halves
    boneless, skinless
4 eggs
1 c. corn starch
1 c. flour

1 c. vinegar
½ c. sugar
½ c. ketchup
1½ c. chicken broth

2 tbsp. soy sauce
1 tsp. salt
1 tsp. ground black peppercorn
3-4 c. vegetable oil

Cut chicken breasts into 1" pieces. Beat eggs in small bowl and set aside. Combine corn starch, flour, salt and pepper in a Ziploc® bag. Dip chicken pieces in egg, place in Ziploc® and coat in flour mixture. In large skillet lightly fry chicken in 3-4 c. vegetable oil, drain chicken and place in 9"x 13" baking dish. In medium saucepan combine soy sauce, ketchup, chicken broth, sugar and vinegar. Bring to a boil. Pour over chicken and bake for 60-70 minutes. Carefully turn chicken pieces every 15 minutes. It's important to turn the chicken and stir the sauce every 15 minutes so the sauce thickens evenly as the chicken bakes. If thinner sauce is desired, add ½-1 c. chicken broth. While chicken is baking, prepare rice and noodles. Just before serving, prepare vegetables. (cont. on right)

Stir Fried Vegetables ⚜

8 oz. pkg. plain Chinese noodles

4 c. sticky rice, uncooked

1 med. red bell pepper

1 med. yellow bell pepper

2 c. snow peas

3 lg. garden carrots

2 green onions

½ tsp. hot chili sesame oil

Prepare both the noodles and the rice according to directions on package and set aside. Slice both bell peppers, dice green onion and snip the ends off the snow peas. Peel carrots and slice them diagonally (as pictured). In wok lightly cook vegetables in hot chili sesame oil.

Prepare plate by placing heaping scoop of rice in center, surround rice with noodles. Surround ball of rice with sweet and sour chicken and garnish with stir fried vegetables. Serve.

Savory Mushroom Stock ⚜

6½ c. water

4 tbsp. granulated chicken bouillon

1 c. mushrooms, thinly sliced

4 green onions

½ tsp. ground black peppercorn

Bring water to a boil, add chicken bouillon and stir until dissolved. Add more bouillon for desired taste. Turn heat on low, fold in mushrooms, gently minced green onions and pepper, simmer for 2-3 minutes. Serve.

❧ Shopping List ❧

each recipe is designed to serve six

chicken breasts, 8 whole boneless, skinless

flank steak, 3 lbs.

spicy ground sausage, 1 lb.

yams, 4 large

baby red potatoes, 5 lbs.

red leaf lettuce, 2 heads

spinach, 10 oz.

carrots, 8 large

green onions, 10

red onion, 1 medium

yellow bell pepper, 1 medium

red bell pepper, 1 medium

snow peas, 4 c.

mushrooms, 1 c.

Roma tomatoes, ¾ c.

fresh basil, 1 c.

fresh ginger, 4 tbsp.

crimson red seedless grapes, 8 c. (4 lbs.)

crisp red apples, 2

limes, 2

blueberries, 2 c.

blackberries, 2 c.

pineapple, 2 c.

raspberries, 2 c.

Parmesan cheese, 1 c. freshly grated

Swiss cheese, 16 oz.

feta cheese, crumbled 5 oz.

cream cheese, 8 oz.

sour cream, 1½ c.

heavy cream, ½ c.

buttermilk, 2 c.

1 baguette

bread, 10 slices
white cooking wine, ¾ c.
raspberry vinegar, ¾ c.
pearl barley, 2 c.
sticky rice, 4 c. uncooked
plain Chinese noodles, 8 oz. pkg.
chicken broth, 4 c. 1½ c.
rye flour, 1 c.
whole wheat flour, 1 c.

yellow cornmeal, 1 c.
corn starch, 1 c.
walnuts, 2 c.
whole pecans, 2½ c.
marshmallow whip, 1 c.
poppy seeds, 1 tbsp.
dry mustard, ¾ tsp.
hot chili sesame oil, ½ tsp.
garlic pepper blend, 1 tsp.

⚜ *Staples* ⚜

flour
milk
eggs
butter
salt
coarse ground black pepper
sugar
brown sugar

granulated chicken bouillon
vegetable oil
extra virgin olive oil
white wine vinegar
balsamic vinegar
ketchup
soy sauce
mayonnaise

honey
maple syrup
vanilla
nutmeg
cinnamon, ground
baking soda
dried oregano
dried chives

CHAPTER FOUR

Gatherings

Week Four
Evening One

Italian Shrimp Pasta

Ocean fresh large sautéed shrimp with garden grown red and
yellow sweet bell peppers, tender green onions and hearty
fettuccine noodles tossed in a creamy white wine butter sauce
finished with fresh ground peppercorns

Italian Style Chop Salad

Fresh crisp lettuce topped with a pinwheel of chopped
Italian delicacies; fresh mozzarella cheese, spicy cured hard
salami, nutty garbanzo beans, aged provolone cheese and
fresh basil drizzled with Italian chop salad dressing

Aged Red Wine Dressing

A zesty purée of garlic cloves, freshly squeezed lemon juice, stone
ground mustard, sweet red onion and savory dried herbs with
aged red wine vinegar and light salad oil

Rosemary Bread

Gently kneaded oven baked bread brushed with creamy
butter and fragrant crushed rosemary, fresh ground black
peppercorns and savory kosher salt

Italian Shrimp Pasta

sauce:

½ c. creamy butter
1 tsp. granulated chicken bouillon
¼ c. flour
½ c. aged white wine
2 c. heavy cream
2 c. 2% milk

In a separate pot, melt butter and granulated bouillon. Add flour and simmer until golden brown. Fold in white wine, cream and milk. Cook for 2-3 minutes. Set aside.

2 lbs. uncooked lg. shrimp
2 tsp. hot sesame oil
1½ med. red bell pepper
1 med. yellow bell pepper
8 green onions

Cook fettuccine noodles al dente. Set aside. Remove tails and skins from uncooked shrimp and rinse. In large wok or skillet on high, drizzle 1 tsp. sesame oil in wok. Sauté shrimp for 2-3 minutes. Cut red and yellow peppers in long strips, add to sautéed shrimp and continue to cook for 2-3 minutes longer. Push shrimp and vegetables to the side and drizzle remaining sesame oil in wok. Add fettuccine noodles and continue to stir fry with shrimp and vegetables. Pour desired amount of sauce in wok, coating evenly. Fold in julienned green onions. Top with fresh ground pepper. Serve immediately.

Italian Style Chop Salad ⚜

2 heads hearts of romaine lettuce

1 can garbanzo beans (15 oz.)

1½ lbs. hard salami

1½ c. provolone cheese

1½ c. fresh mozzarella cheese (in water)

2 med. red bell peppers

1 c. fresh basil, gently minced

Wash and tear lettuce in bite size pieces and place in fridge to chill before serving. Chop hard salami, provolone cheese, mozzarella cheese and bell pepper. Place chopped lettuce in bowls, add about ¼ c. of salami, provolone cheese, mozzarella cheese, bell peppers and drained garbanzo beans divided in sections over the top of lettuce and top with minced basil in the center. Cover and refrigerate until ready to serve. (Pictured in individual serving bowls.)

Aged Red Wine Dressing ⚜

½ c. red wine vinegar

1 lemon

1 tbsp. stone ground mustard

3 garlic cloves, minced

¼ sweet red onion

1 tbsp. dried chives

2 tsp. dried oregano

2 tbsp. sugar

¾ c. vegetable oil

¼ c. Karo™ syrup

½ tsp. sea salt

1 tbsp. black pepper

Gently squeeze juice of 1 lemon in blender. Combine all other ingredients and purée. Chill.

Rosemary Bread ⚜

2¾ c. flour

1 tsp. sea salt

1 tsp. sugar

1 tbsp. active dry yeast

1 tbsp. vegetable oil

1 c. water

1 tbsp. garlic powder

1 egg white

1-2 tsp. extra virgin olive oil

2 tbsp. kosher salt

1 tsp. coarse black pepper

2 tbsp. rosemary, crushed

Preheat oven to 450°. Whisk together 2¾ c flour, salt, sugar, yeast and garlic powder. Mix well. Fold in oil and water with a fork. Place on a lightly floured surface and need dough for 6 minutes until it is resilient but smooth. Divide dough into 6 round balls. Place on a large cookie sheet far enough apart that they will not touch if they double in size. Brush with olive oil and cover with a thin towel in a warm place for 30 minutes. When dough has doubled in size, brush with lightly beaten egg white and sprinkle with a mix of kosher salt, black pepper and rosemary. Snip the very top of the small loaf as well as the four corners of each small loaf with scissors for a decorative look. Bake at 450° for 12-15 minutes until golden brown. Serve warm.

Notes & Comments

Gatherings

Week Four
Evening Two

Chicken Stroganoff

Tender shredded chicken folded into a light and creamy
herb sauce served on a bed of warm rice, topped with gently diced
fresh sweet red bell peppers

Toasted Cheese Bread

An open faced oven roasted baguette completed with our
flavorful garlic cheese spread broiled to perfection

Date Salad

Sun sweetened dates, gently sautéed applewood bacon combined
with a refreshing blend of colorful garden fresh vegetables tossed in
our light Sweet Poppy Seed Dressing

Broccoli Souffle

This warm blend of broccoli and Roquefort cheese
is spiced to perfection and is polished with buttery seasoned bread
crumbs for an inviting crisp texture

Chicken Stroganoff

4 chicken breasts, boneless, skinless

2 c. sour cream

2 c. cream of chicken soup

1 c. 1% milk

1/8 tsp. dried dill

1/2 tsp. garlic salt

1/2 tsp. onion salt

1/2 red bell pepper

3 c. white rice

1 tsp. chicken bouillon

Using cooking spray, lightly salt and pepper chicken breasts, add 1/3 c. of water, let chicken simmer for 20 minutes. Cool. Using two forks, shred tender chicken into bite size pieces, set aside. Combine sour cream, soup and seasonings. Pour in milk. As the sauce begins to heat, fold in the shredded chicken. Prepare rice according to directions, substituting granulated chicken bouillon for salt. Serve white rice topped with stroganoff, garnished with diced red bell pepper and freshly ground black peppercorns.

Date Salad

1 head iceberg lettuce

1 head hearts of romaine lettuce

1 med. yellow bell pepper

1 med. red bell pepper

3/4 c. dates, chopped

1 lb. smoked bacon

Chop bacon in small pieces, lightly sauté until tender, set aside. Rinse and chop fresh vegetables and lettuce. Dice dates, toss together with bacon. Top with Sweet Poppy Seed Dressing. (pg. 73)

Toasted Cheese Bread ⚜

1 loaf French bread or baguette
½ c. butter softened

1 c. Asiago cheese
1 c. Jack cheese, shredded

1 c. mayonnaise
½ clove garlic, minced

Fold butter, cheeses, garlic and mayonnaise together and spread over slices of bread. Broil for 1–2 minutes.

Broccoli Souffle ⚜

2 lbs. fresh broccoli

1 yellow onion

½ tsp. Tabasco™ sauce

3 eggs

3 tbsp. flour

½ c. seasoned dry bread crumbs

4 oz. Roquefort cheese

1 c. hot 2% milk

1 c. grated sharp cheddar

2 tbsp. butter

½ tsp. salt

Preheat oven to 350°. Bring 4 c. of water to a boil. When preparing broccoli, discard most of the stem (as pictured), place broccoli in pot and blanch for 1 minute. Do not overcook. Remove from water, rinse and set aside. Sauté butter and minced onions in a skillet, cook until tender. Whisk in flour and let cook for 1 minute. Slowly add milk and whisk. Cook until it thickens, stirring constantly. Remove from heat, stir in cheddar cheese, Tabasco™ sauce and salt. Let cool. In a separate bowl, beat eggs and stir into the cooled cheese mixture. Fold in broccoli, top with breadcrumbs and Roquefort cheese bake for 30 minutes.

Gatherings ⚜
Week Four
Evening Three

Traditional Lasagna

Rich, satisfying layers of hearty lasagna noodles,
traditional creamy cheeses, savory ground beef and Italian herb
marinara sauce baked until flavors perfectly
meld together in this classic favorite

Italian Lasagna Sauce

A family favorite with a creamy twist: browned ground beef,
sautéed yellow onion, garden fresh herbs and cream cheese
simmered in chunky stewed Italian tomatoes

Spinach & Bell Pepper Salad

Fresh tender baby spinach topped with garden fresh red and yellow
bell peppers, plump cherry tomatoes and sweet red
onion rings drizzled with a cheesy aged balsamic vinaigrette

Sweet Tomato Basil Bread

Oven fresh bread with a baked-in crust of aged Parmesan cheese,
sweet cherry tomatoes, fresh basil and tender yellow
onion with a dash of savory thyme

Traditional Lasagna ⚜

12 oz. ricotta cheese

16 oz. box of lasagna noodles

2 tbsp. extra virgin olive oil

1 tsp. kosher salt

12 oz. cottage cheese

1½ lbs. grated mozzarella cheese

2 green onions

Preheat oven to 375°. In a large stock pot combine oil and salt and cook lasagna noodles al dente. Using an extra deep 9"x 13" pan, spread Italian Lasagna Sauce evenly on bottom of the pan, place three or four lasagna noodles on sauce. Using teaspoons, alternate heaping spoonfuls of ricotta cheese and cottage cheese. Place every two to three inches apart. Top with tomato sauce and 1 c. of mozzarella cheese. Cover with another layer of noodles and repeat steps. Finish with sauce and mozzarella cheese. Cover with aluminum foil and bake for 45 minutes. Remove foil and bake an additional 15 minutes. Top with fresh diced green onions.

Italian Lasagna Sauce ⚜

1 yellow onion

1 tbsp. extra virgin olive oil

8 oz. cream cheese

2 cans tomato paste (14.5 oz. ea.)

3 c. water

1 tsp. oregano, dried

¾ c. chopped basil

1 tsp. onion salt

1 tsp. black pepper

2 lbs. ground beef

1 tsp. garlic powder

¾ c. sugar

2 fresh bay leaves

3 cans stewed Italian style tomatoes (14.5 oz. ea.)

Sauté diced onion in olive oil, cook until onions are clear. Add 1 can stewed tomatoes, half of the sugar and bay leaves, sauté for 10 minutes. Place in blender two cans stewed tomatoes, other half of sugar, oregano, basil, garlic powder, water and tomato paste. Blend thoroughly. Fold into tomato sauce, simmer for 30 minutes. Brown ground beef with onion salt, fold in cream cheese until melted and combine with tomato sauce. *Helpful Hint: This traditional sauce can be used as a base for other Italian pasta dishes: three cheese tortellini, stuffed manicotti or home style spaghetti.*

Spinach & Bell Pepper Salad

20 oz. bag spinach
1 med. yellow bell pepper
1 med. orange bell pepper
½ med. red onion
1 ½ c. cherry tomatoes

Wash spinach and chill. Slice peppers in rings. Slice red onion in half circles. Fold in cherry tomatoes and toss with crisp spinach. Top with Balsamic Cheese Dressing and serve.

Balsamic Cheese Dressing

½ c. drained cottage cheese
½ c. balsamic vinegar
½ c. light Karo™ syrup
½ c. vegetable oil
1 tsp. dried mustard
½ tsp. salt
½ tsp. pepper

Mix all ingredients except cottage cheese in blender, fold in drained cottage cheese and whisk together. Chill and serve.

Sweet Tomato Basil Bread ⚜

2¾ c. all-purpose flour
1 tsp. salt
2 tbsp. sugar
1 tbsp. active dry yeast
1 tbsp. vegetable oil
1 c. water
1 tsp. garlic powder
¼ tsp. thyme

¼ c. dried Parmesan cheese
1 c. sliced cherry tomatoes
¼ c. chopped fresh basil
2 tsp. sugar
½ tsp. coarse black pepper
2 tsp. extra virgin olive oil
½ yellow onion diced

Preheat oven to 450°. In a medium size bowl, mix flour, 2 tbsp. sugar, yeast and garlic powder together with a wire whisk. Fold in oil and water with a fork. Dough will be crumbly but turn onto floured surface scraping all dough from bowl and knead about 5 minutes. Dough will become smooth. Brush with extra virgin olive oil and place back in bowl, cover with moist towel in a warm place. Let rise for half an hour. Carefully pick up ball of dough and lightly stretch it into a square while placing it on a large cookie sheet. Be careful not to flatten bread dough. Brush with olive oil. Evenly spread diced onion, chopped basil, dried thyme and Parmesan cheese on the bread. Slice cherry tomatoes and place evenly on bread and sprinkle with 2 tsp. sugar, salt and pepper. Bake in preheated oven for 15 minutes or until golden brown. Serve warm.

❦ Notes & Comments ❦

Gatherings ⚜

Week Four
Evening Four

Rib Eye Pot Pie

Golden brown flaky pastry pockets filled with tender
sautéed chunks of rib eye steak and garden fresh diced
vegetables in a rich savory brown gravy

Chicken Pot Pie

Tender chicken breast and diced potatoes in a rich creamy cheese
sauce with garden fresh zucchini, sweet red bell pepper and
sultry mushrooms in a flaky homemade crust

Spinach & Mushroom Salad

Traditional fresh baby spinach leaves, thinly sliced mushrooms, gently minced garden fresh red onion, sweet red bell pepper
topped with creamy cottage cheese finished with
chilled Sweet Apple Cider Dressing

Zucchini Bread

Cinnamon, nutmeg and cloves combined with hearty garden
zucchini highlight the flavors of this sweet satisfying bread

Chocolate Banana Bread

A sumptuous dessert bread with the distinctive sweetness of fresh
ripe bananas and deep rich chocolate

Rib Eye Pot Pie ⚜

2 lbs. rib eye steak

1 tsp. extra virgin olive oil

1 c. diced carrots

1 c. diced green beans

¼ c. green onions

8 oz. square cream cheese

1½ tsp. granulated beef bouillon

2 pkg. brown gravy mix. (1 c. ea.)

1 egg white

2 c. diced potatoes

Cut rib eye steak into small chunks, sauté in olive oil for 2-3 minutes stirring regularly, set aside. Prepare diced carrots, green beans and potatoes and combine with cream cheese and granulated beef bouillon. Prepare one brown gravy mix according to package instructions, fold into cream cheese and vegetable mixture. Add rib eye steak with drippings from the pan and mix filling well.

Pastry ⚜

| 3 c. flour | 1½ tsp. salt | 1 c.+ 2 tbsp. shortening | 9-10 tbsp. ice water | 1 egg white |

Preheat oven to 425°. Sift flour and salt together, cut in shortening with pastry blender until pieces are the size of small peas. Sprinkle ice water over dough, gently mix forming ten small balls of pastry. Turn onto a floured surface, handling as little as possible. With a rolling pin, roll out dough in oval shape. Place ¼ c. filling in center of pastry. Brush edges with egg white. Fold over and pinch edges to seal tightly. Brush tops with egg white and sprinkle with kosher salt. Bake for 12-15 minutes or until golden brown. Prepare beef gravy as per packet instructions. Drizzle over beef pot pies. Top with diced green onions.

Chicken Pot Pie ⚜

3 chicken breasts, boneless, skinless

3 tbsp. butter

6 oz. cream cheese

3 tbsp. olive oil

¾ tsp. pepper

2 tsp. granulated chicken bouillon

½ c. med. red bell pepper

⅔ c. mushrooms

3 med. Yukon potatoes

1 zucchini

3 tbsp. flour

1 tsp. kosher salt

Heat olive oil on high in a large skillet. Sauté lightly salted chicken breasts until tender. Dice chicken, sprinkle with flour and combine with skillet drippings, set aside. Cream together softened butter and cream cheese, add pepper and granulated chicken bouillon to cooked chicken. Cut zucchini in fourths and remove seeds and chop. Fold in diced red bell peppers, sliced mushrooms, chopped zucchini and diced potatoes. Fold into chicken pie filling.

Pastry ⚜

| 2 c. flour | 1 tsp. salt | ¾ c. shortening | 6-7 tbsp. ice water | 1 egg white |

Preheat oven to 425°. Sift flour and salt together, cut in shortening with pastry blender until pieces are the size of small peas. Sprinkle ice water over dough, gently mix forming two medium size balls of pastry. Turn onto a floured surface, handling as little

as possible. On a lightly floured surface carefully roll out bottom shell, place in 9" pie pan. Leaving enough pastry to hang over the edge. Generously fill pie shell with chicken filling. Roll out other half of pastry, fold in half. Make small cuts in pastry lid, place on top, pinch edges, brush pastry lid with lightly beaten egg white and finish with kosher salt. Bake for 45 minutes until golden brown.

Spinach & Mushroom Salad ⚜

20 oz. bag fresh spinach	1 sm. red onion
2 c. sliced mushrooms	1½ c. low fat cottage cheese, drained
1 lg. red bell pepper	

Clean and slice fresh mushrooms. Chop red onion in very small pieces. Dice red bell pepper and toss with rinsed spinach. Just before serving drain cottage cheese in a colander and fold into salad. Top with Sweet Apple Cider Dressing and serve.

Sweet Apple Cider Dressing ⚜

½ c. water	⅔ c. apple cider vinegar	1 tsp. salt
1½ c. vegetable oil	2 tsp. dry mustard	1 tsp. coarse pepper
1¼ c. sugar		

Combine all ingredients and mix well, chill before serving.

Chocolate Banana Bread ⚜

⅓ c. shortening
½ c. sugar
2 eggs

1 ¾ c. flour
1 tsp. baking powder
½ tsp. baking soda

½ tsp. salt
1 c. mashed ripe bananas
1 c. semi-sweet chocolate chips

Preheat oven to 350°. Cream shortening and sugar together until fluffy, add eggs and mix well. In separate bowl sift together dry ingredients. Fold in a small portion of dry ingredients, then add a portion of mashed bananas. Continue alternating the dry ingredients and the bananas into the sugar mixture until complete. Fold in chocolate chips. Do not over mix. Bake for 30-40 minutes. Makes two small loaves.

Zucchini Bread ⚜

3 c. flour
1 tbsp. cinnamon
¼ tsp. cloves
¼ tsp. nutmeg
1 tsp. salt
1 c. sugar
1 c. brown sugar
1 tsp. baking soda
¼ tsp. baking powder
3 eggs
1 c. vegetable oil
1 tsp. vanilla
2 c. grated zucchini

Preheat oven to 325°. Combine flour, cinnamon, cloves, nutmeg, salt, baking soda and baking powder together and set aside. Beat eggs, sugar, brown sugar, vegetable oil and vanilla. Slowly mix in dry ingredients. Add dry ingredients to mixture and fold in grated zucchini. Pour into two greased 8"x 4" loaf tins. Bake for 50-60 minutes. Makes two large loaves.

❧ *Shopping List* ❧

each recipe is designed to serve six

chicken breasts, 7 whole boneless, skinless

smoked bacon, 1 lb.

shrimp, 2 lbs large uncooked

hard salami, 1½ lbs.

ground beef, 2 lbs

rib eye steak, 2 lbs.

French bread, 1 loaf or baguette

white rice, 3 c.

potatoes, 6 medium

iceberg lettuce, 1 head

hearts of romaine lettuce, 3 heads

spinach, 2 bags (20 oz. ea.)

mushrooms, 3 c.

cherry tomatoes, 2½ c.

green onions, 12

yellow onion, 3 medium

red onion, 2 medium

zucchini, 3 medium

red bell peppers, 7 medium

yellow bell pepper, 2 medium

orange bell pepper, 1 medium

carrots, 1 c.

green beans, 1 c.

very ripe bananas, 2

lemon, 1

dates, ¾ c.

fresh broccoli, 2 lbs.

fresh basil, 2 c.

fresh bay leaves

fresh garlic, 4 cloves

sour cream, 2 c.

heavy cream, 2 c.

cream cheese, 22 oz.

cottage cheese, 3½ c.

ricotta cheese, 12 oz.

mozzarella cheese, 1½ lbs.

fresh mozzarella cheese (in water), 1½ c.

dried Parmesan cheese, ¼ c.

sharp cheddar, 1 c.

Roquefort cheese, 4 oz.

provolone cheese, 1½ c.

Monterey Jack cheese, 1 c.

Asiago cheese, 1 c.

Karo™ syrup, ¾ c.

white cooking wine, ½ c.

red wine vinegar, ½ c.

apple cider vinegar, ⅓ c.

active dry yeast, 2 tbsp.

semi-sweet chocolate chips, 1 c.

seasoned dry bread crumbs, ½ c.

stone ground mustard, 1 tbsp.

garbanzo beans, 1 can (15 oz.)

cream of chicken soup, 2 c.

tomato paste, 2 cans (14.5 oz. ea.)

Italian Style stewed tomatoes, 3 cans (14.5 oz. ea.)

Ranch Dressing Mix or see (pg. 188)

brown gravy mix, 2 pkg. (.87 oz. ea.)

Tabasco™, ½ tsp.

hot sesame oil, 2 tsp.

lasagna noodles, 16 oz.

⚜ *Staples* ⚜

flour	extra virgin olive oil	dried chives,
milk	balsamic vinegar	dried oregano
eggs	mayonnaise	dried thyme
butter	vanilla	dried mustard
kosher salt	baking soda	garlic powder
coarse black pepper	baking powder	onion salt
sugar	ground cinnamon	granulated chicken bouillon
brown sugar	cloves, ¼ tsp.	granulated beef bouillon
shortening	nutmeg	
vegetable oil	rosemary, crushed	

CHAPTER FIVE

Gatherings ⚜

Week Five
Evening One

Ginger Glazed Salmon

Seared market fresh salmon filet glazed in a sophisticated
fresh ginger, honey and rice wine vinegar reduction

Baby Basil Potatoes

Naturally delicious baby new potatoes steamed until tender and
tossed with garden fresh gently minced basil leaves and
sweet creamy butter

Bacon Sugar Snap Peas

Crisp green sugar snap peas, hickory smoked bacon
with sweet yellow onions lightly sautéed

Shelley's Famous Scones

Decadent melt in your mouth fried fluffy pastries served warm
with sweet and creamy honey butter

Shelley's Honey Butter

Whipped creamy butter blended with sweet fresh honey
and marshmallow fluff

Ginger Glazed Salmon ⚜

2 lbs. salmon fillet
2 tsp. extra virgin olive oil
1 tsp. kosher salt

Cut large salmon fillet into desired pieces. In a heavy skillet heat olive oil and salt
on high until a drop of water splatters in
oil. Take each fillet and place skin down
in skillet searing the salmon quickly. Let
it cook covered for 4-6 minutes. Turn
over and remove skin, continue to sauté
for an additional 4-6 minutes, without
lid, until golden brown. Drizzle with
glaze and serve immediately.

Ginger Glaze ⚜

2 tbsp. extra virgin olive oil
¼ c. minced fresh ginger
½ onion, minced

¼ c. balsamic vinegar
1½ c. honey
⅔ c. rice vinegar
2 tsp. salt
¼ c. light Karo™ syrup

In a small skillet sauté olive oil, salt, ginger and minced onion for 2-3 minutes. Stir in rice vinegar, honey, balsamic vinegar and Karo™ syrup. Bring
to a boil and turn down heat, let simmer to a reduction for 6-8 minutes.
Sauce will thicken as it sits. *Helpful Hint: This glaze is also great with chicken,
shrimp or beef.*

Baby Basil Potatoes ⚜

2 lbs. baby new potatoes
1/3 c. butter melted
1/3 c. minced fresh basil
2 tbsp. kosher salt

Wash and clean baby new potatoes. Prick each potato two or three times so they will absorb the savory salty flavor. Place in a medium size pot with hot water and 2 tbsp. of kosher salt. Bring to a boil and let simmer for 20 minutes checking to not over cook. Drain water and toss with melted butter and fresh basil. Serve immediately.

Bacon Sugar Snap Peas ⚜

1/2 lb. bacon
1/2 med. yellow onion
4 c. sugar snap peas

In a heavy skillet place diced bacon and begin to sauté. Cook for 2–3 minutes, add diced onion. Continue to sauté until bacon is crisp and onions are golden. Remove bacon grease and stir in snap peas and continue cooking for 1–2 minutes until peas are heated completely. Peas should remain crisp. Serve immediately.

Shelley's Famous Scones ⚜

2 c. warm water
2 tbsp. yeast
2 tbsp. sugar
¼ c. shortening
2 eggs
2 tsp. salt
5½ c. flour
4 c. vegetable oil

Sprinkle yeast and sugar in bowl of warm water. Let sit 5 minutes, mix in remaining ingredients. Turn onto a floured surface and knead by hand for 5-6 minutes. Return to bowl, cover with damp cloth and let dough rise for 30 minutes. Separate dough in half and roll into a rectangle about ¼" thick and cut into desired size. In a large pot on high, heat oil until it pops. Place each piece of dough in hot oil and turn when golden brown. Repeat with other half of dough.

Shelley's Honey Butter ⚜

¼ c. butter
¾ c. honey
¾ c. marshmallow whip

Whip butter until light. Add honey and fold in marshmallow whip. Blend together and serve. Refrigerate left over honey butter.

Strawberry Kiwi Salad ⚜

3 ripe avocados

6 kiwis

3 c. sliced strawberries

2 med. oranges

1-2 heads hearts of romaine lettuce

Clean and shred lettuce, chill. Slice strawberries, peel and slice kiwis in whole circles. Cut avocado in half moon slices. Peel orange and slice in circles. Break apart in sections. Toss everything together and garnish salad with dressing to taste, just before serving.

Orange Lime Dressing ⚜

½ c. oil

juice of 4 limes

½ c. sugar

1 tsp. orange zest

Gently squeeze four fresh limes, fold in oil and sugar. Using the rind of an orange freshly grate 1 tsp. of zest. Blend together. Chill. Garnish salad with dressing to taste.

Gatherings ⚜
Week Five
Evening Two

Chicken Crepes

This breakfast favorite is hearty enough to satisfy
every appetite any time of the day. Delicate egg crepes filled with a
cheesy blend of herb creamed tender chicken breast, buttery
sautéed mushrooms with garden onions,
sweet bell peppers and aged Swiss cheese

Pastry Wrapped Sausages

An old family treasure everyone will enjoy. Flaky
homemade pastry wrapped around lightly sautéed mild
sausage links and baked to a golden finish

Fresh Fruit

Chilled fresh peak-season berries and banana slices combine to
create a sweet fruit salad to complete this meal

Chicken Crepes ⚜

filling:

3 c. cooked chicken breasts

1 tbsp. creamy butter

1 c. sliced mushrooms

½ med. yellow onion

1 c. sour cream

2 c. grated Swiss cheese

½ med. red bell pepper

1 can cream of chicken soup (14.5 oz.)

2 green onions

1 tsp. onion salt

½ tsp. coarse pepper

Fresh peak season berries and bananas

Sauté sliced mushrooms, minced onions and diced red bell pepper in butter until cooked. Add sour cream, onion salt, pepper and soup. Fold in shredded chicken breasts, cook on medium heat for 2-3 minutes. Fill crepes with chicken filling, top with grated cheese and roll (as pictured). Top with chicken filling, garnish with Swiss cheese and minced green onions. Serve immediately.

Crepes ⚜

6 eggs

¾ c. 2% milk

¾ c. chicken stock

3 tbsp. melted butter

¾ tsp. salt

1½ c. flour

Beat eggs in large dish. Combine milk, chicken stock, melted butter and salt. Blend in flour using medium speed. Let stand 1 hour at room temperature. Heat crepe maker, dip in batter. Cook 1-1½ minutes, makes 20-24 crepes.

Pastry Wrapped Sausages ⚜

30 plump sausages

Brown sausages lightly in skillet. When all sausages are seared on all sides, pour ¾ c. water over them and cover with a lid. Let steam for 6–8 minutes turning occasionally. Let cool to the touch, wrap with pastry and bake. Pastry Wrapped Sausages can be made ahead of time and kept covered in the refrigerator and baked fresh when ready to serve.

Pastry ⚜

| 2 c. flour | 1 tsp. salt | ¾ c. shortening | 6–7 tbsp. ice water | 1 egg white |

Preheat oven to 425°. Sift flour and salt together, cut in shortening with pastry blender until pieces are the size of small peas. Sprinkle ice water over dough, gently mix together. Turn onto a floured surface, handling as little as possible. Form small balls the size of a large tangerine. With a rolling pin, roll out dough into a rectangle shape. Using a knife cut into thin strips. Wrap each cooked sausage with pastry strip (as pictured). Place on cookie sheet, brush pastry with beaten egg white and bake for 10–12 minutes or until pastry is golden.

Gatherings
Week Five
Evening Three

Asian Chicken Salad

Freshly fried rice noodles are a classic accompaniment
to this Asian chicken salad. Gently shredded Napa cabbage, with
tender pieces of torn chicken breast, sweet marinated red bell
pepper strips and crisp fresh snow peas complete with an authentic
sweet Toasted Sesame Dressing for a classic Asian taste

Toasted Sesame Dressing

Natural rice wine vinegar and oil sweetened and blended with
ginger, seasonings and toasted sesame seeds

Avocado Egg Rolls

Crisp egg rolls stuffed with fresh ripe avocado and sweet bay shrimp
seasoned with hot chili pepper and fresh cilantro

Pot Stickers

Colorful Chinese vegetables and spicy ground sausage filled wonton
triangles sauteed until lightly browned and steamed. Served with
a fresh cilantro lime dipping sauce

Toasted Sesame Dressing ⚜

½ tsp. ginger	4 tbsp. oil
3 tbsp. rice vinegar	5 tbsp. sugar
2 tsp. salt	2 tsp. Accent™
3 tbsp. apple cider vinegar	2 tsp. toasted sesame seeds

Combine all dressing ingredients, except sesame seeds, in blender and mix on high. Fold in sesame seeds. Cut red bell peppers into thin slices and marinate in half of the salad dressing for a few hours if possible.

Asian Chicken Salad ⚜

6 chicken breasts, boneless, skinless	1 pkg. Maifun™ rice sticks (6.75 oz.)	12 oz. snow peas
2 med. red bell peppers	1 head Chinese cabbage	2 c. vegetable oil
8 green onions	1 tsp. fresh ground pepper	

Prepare a pot using cooking spray, lightly salt and pepper chicken breasts and place in a covered pot on medium heat. If chicken is frozen they will cook in their own juices. (If not frozen add ⅓ cup of water so chicken can simmer.) Heat vegetable oil in skillet on high, break rice noodles into four sections and quickly add to hot oil. Rice noodles will cook quickly and expand. Place rice noodles on a paper towel to drain excess oil. Repeat for all noodles. Shred Chinese cabbage, dice onions and cut chicken. Toss together with rice noodles and snow peas. Fold in marinated red bell peppers with dressing, toss together. Add more dressing as desired. Top with fresh ground pepper.

Pot Stickers

1 lb. ground sausage

¼ head purple cabbage

3 c. shredded cabbage

3 lg. carrots

3 green onions

2 c. chicken broth

1 tsp. soy sauce

½ tsp. pepper

1 egg white

3 c. cooking oil

¾ tsp. hot chili sesame oil

1 pkg. wonton wrappers

Sauté ground sausage until fully cooked. Add shredded purple and green cabbage. Dice green onions, grate carrots and fold into sausage mix. Take a wonton wrapper, brush the outside edge with egg white. Fill the middle with about 1 tbsp. of mixture. Fold in half diagonally pressing edges tightly together. Repeat. Drizzle hot chili sesame oil in frying pan, move oil around with spatula, place pot stickers on sides and sauté until lightly browned with crisp edges. Turn over and repeat. Pour ½ cup chicken broth in pan and quickly cover, allowing pot stickers to steam until all liquid is gone. Serve immediately.

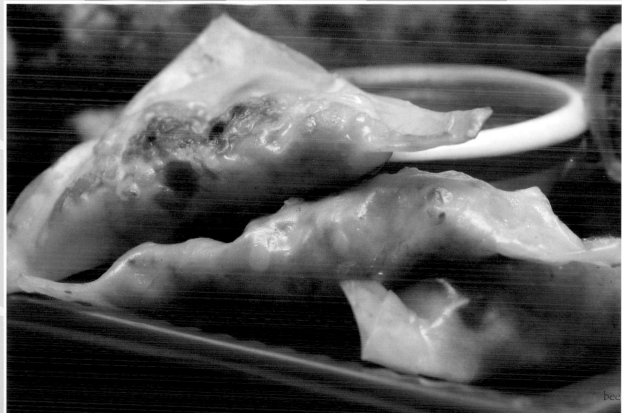

Avocado Egg Roll ⚜

3 ripe avocados

2 c. bay shrimp

½ c. cilantro

½ tsp. crushed hot chili pepper

1 ½ c. cooked Maifun™ rice sticks

1 egg white

3 c. cooking oil

1 pkg. egg roll wrappers

Mash ripe avocados leaving chunks. Fold in shrimp, cilantro, chili pepper and noodles. Lightly beat egg white. Using an egg roll wrapper, fill middle of wrapper with 2-3 tbsp. avocado filling. Fold in the sides and roll sealing the ends with egg white. Repeat. In a shallow skillet heat cooking oil (test with piece of egg roll wrapper for a quick fry). Place egg rolls in oil until golden, turn only once. Place on a paper towel to absorb excess oil. Serve immediately.

Cilantro Lime Dipping Sauce ⚜

5 tbsp. Karo™ syrup

5 tbsp. sugar

2 bunches fresh cilantro

¼ tsp. salt

juice of 6 limes, ½ c.

Put all ingredients in blender and mix together. Makes 10 oz. Store in a covered container in fridge.

❧ Notes & Comments ❧

Gatherings ⚜
Week Five
Evening Four

Maggie's Marinated Burgers

Deeply marinated ground Kobe beef in a blend of savory
seasonings for a full flavor, then grilled medium rare and dressed
out with cheddar cheese and fresh jalapeño salsa

Toasted Sesame Asparagus

Tender oven roasted fresh green asparagus spears sprinkled with salt,
ground pepper and nutty sesame seeds

Jalapeño Hamburger Salsa

Hot, spicy jalapeño relish with chopped ripe red tomato, fresh
cilantro, minced white onion and tangy fresh squeezed lime

Bleu Cheese Potato Chips

Wafer thin fresh fried potato chips sprinkled with a blend of kosher
salt, crumbled bleu cheese and aged Parmesan

Mozzarella Spinach Salad

A medley of color and texture: soft white mozzarella balls, crisp
purple cabbage, tender green baby spinach, sweet red bell pepper,
delicate mushroom slices and crunchy roasted pepitas
finished with a silky Sweet Basil Dressing

Maggie's Marinated Burgers ⚜

2 lbs. Kobe ground beef
Worcestershire sauce
seasoned pepper
garlic salt
hamburger seasoning
Hot Shot™ Black and Red Pepper

Form ¼ lb. burgers and line a 9" x 13" pan with patties. Drizzle 1 tsp. of Worcestershire sauce on each burger. Generously season each burger with seasoned pepper, garlic salt and hamburger seasoning. Top with a few shakes of Hot Shot™ and turn burgers over and repeat on the other side. Let sit in fridge for 2 days or at least overnight. Cook on grill turning two to three times until medium rare. Top with cheese and Jalapeño Hamburger Salsa. Add barbecue sauce. Serve immediately.

Barbecue Sauce ⚜

1 can tomato paste (8 oz.)	½ tsp. pepper
1 can tomato sauce (8 oz.)	2 tbsp. apple cider vinegar
3 cloves garlic	2 tbsp. extra virgin olive oil
1 tbsp. Worcestershire sauce	½ c. sugar
1 tsp. ground dry mustard	2 tbsp. dark molasses
1 tsp. cayenne pepper	

Cook garlic and onion in olive oil until it is soft. Add all other ingredients. Simmer on low for 20-30 minutes. Keep stirring it often so it doesn't burn. Refrigerate for a few days. For hamburger sauce add ⅓ c. mayonnaise to 1 c. Barbecue sauce. *Helpful Hint: This sauce is great for chicken or pulled pork sandwiches.*

Toasted Sesame Asparagus ⚜

2 bundles fresh asparagus
3 tbs. sesame seeds
2 tbsp. extra virgin olive oil

1 tsp. kosher salt
½ tsp. coarse black pepper

Preheat oven to 425°. Clean asparagus and cut off bottom inch. Spread on cookie sheet and brush with olive oil. Sprinkle with sesame seeds, salt and pepper. Bake for 8-10 minutes, turn asparagus over and bake for additional 8-10 minutes. Serve immediately..

Jalapeño Hamburger Salsa ⚜

1 fresh lime
½ green bell pepper
¼ c. cilantro, minced
1 jalapeño

1 tomato
½ white onion
1 tsp. pepper
1 tsp. salt

Finely chop bell pepper, tomato, onion, cilantro and jalapeño into small chunks and combine in bowl with salt and pepper. Squeeze the juice of one lime over the top, toss and refrigerate. Serve on cheeseburger.

Bleu Cheese Potato Chips ⚜

6 med. size potatoes

1 qt. vegetable oil

½ c. dry Parmesan cheese

½ c. crumbled bleu cheese

1 tsp. kosher salt

In large soup pot heat oil on high until a potato slice pops quickly in oil. Slice potatoes with a peeler in very thin slices. Combine salt, Parmesan cheese and bleu cheese together in a bowl to create cheese seasoning mix. Drop handfuls of potato slices in hot oil and quickly fry chips. Stir gently to separate chips. Remove from oil, spread on a paper towel lined baking tray. Sprinkle with cheese seasoning mix. Repeat until all potatoes are cooked. Serve immediately or keep in a warm 200° oven until ready to serve.

Mozzarella Spinach Salad ⚜

20 oz. bag of baby spinach

¾ c. med. red bell pepper, diced

2 c. baby mozzarella balls

½ c. chopped purple cabbage

3 c. sliced fresh mushrooms

1 c. roasted and salted pepitas *(roasted and salted shelled pumpkin or squash seeds)*

Toss clean spinach with sliced mushrooms, red bell pepper, purple cabbage and mozzarella balls. Fold in pepitas and finish with Sweet Basil Dressing.

Sweet Basil Dressing ⚜

½ c. fresh squeezed lime juice
(juice of 6 fresh limes)

⅔ c. vegetable oil

1 c. sugar

1 c. white wine vinegar

¾ c. fresh basil, minced

½ tsp. pepper

1 tsp. kosher salt

Mix together in a blender. Chill.

⚜ Shopping List ⚜

each recipe is designed to serve six

salmon fillets, 2 lbs.
bay shrimp, ½ c.
Kobe ground beef, 2 lbs.
smoked bacon, ½ lb.
ground sausage, 1 lb.
chicken breasts, 9 whole boneless, skinless
breakfast sausages, 30
baby new potatoes, 2 lbs.
potatoes, 6 medium
hearts of romaine lettuce, 1 head
baby spinach, 20 oz. bag
jalapeño, 1
ripe avocados, 5
fresh asparagus, 2 bundles
Chinese cabbage, 1 head
cabbage, 1 c. shredded
purple cabbage, ½ head
snow peas, 12 oz.
white onion, 2 medium

yellow onion, ½ medium
green onions, 11
tomato, 1 large
carrots, 3 large
mushrooms, 4 c. sliced
red bell pepper, 4 medium
green bell pepper, 1 medium
sugar snap peas, 4 c.
fresh basil, 1¼ c.
fresh cilantro, ¾ c.
fresh ginger, 2 tbsp.
garlic, 3 cloves
limes, 17
kiwis, 4
strawberries, 2 c.
orange, 1 large
marshmallow whip, ¾ c.
rice wine vinegar, 1¼ c.
apple cider vinegar, 5 tbsp.

wonton wrappers, 1 pkg.

egg roll wrappers, 1 pkg.

Maifun™ rice sticks, 2 pkg (6.75 oz.)

hot chili sesame oil

toasted sesame seeds, 2 tsp.

chicken stock, 2½ c.

cream of chicken soup, 1 can (10¾ oz.)

tomato paste, 1 can (8 oz.)

tomato sauce, 1 can (8 oz.)

buttermilk, 1 c.

Swiss cheese, 2 c. grated

bleu cheese, ½ c. crumbled

baby mozzarella balls, 2 c.

Parmesan cheese, ½ c. dry

sour cream, 1 c.

hamburger seasoning

Hot Shot™ Black and Red Pepper

roasted and salted pepitas, 1 c.

Karo™ syrup, 2 tbsp.

dark molasses, 2 tbsp.

❧ Staples ❧

flour

milk

eggs

butter

shortening

kosher salt

coarse black pepper

sugar

vegetable oil

extra virgin olive oil

balsamic vinegar

white wine vinegar

honey

soy sauce

baking powder

baking soda

onion salt

ginger

Accent™

crushed hot chili pepper

ground dry mustard

sesame seeds

mayonnaise

Worcestershire Sauce

seasoned pepper

garlic Salt

cayenne pepper

CHAPTER SIX

❧ Effortless Dishes ❧

Karl's Famous Breakfast Burritos

Tender green chilies and fluffy scrambled eggs, blended with spicy ground sausage
folded in a warm flour tortilla with shredded cheddar cheese, topped with jalapeño hot sauce
and finished with a dollop of sour cream to put out the fire

Chicken a la King

Freshly baked flaky pastry shells filled with tender shredded pieces of savory chicken
and blended together in a light creamy sauce with sweet young green peas,
this traditional meal is a family favorite.

Chicken Rosemary

Oven roasted layers of tender white chicken breast, marinated artichoke hearts and fresh sautéed mushrooms in a light sauce of fresh aromatic rosemary and Parmesan spooned over wild rice

Pulled Pork Quesadilla

Crisp flour tortillas filled with Colby Jack cheese and sweet and spicy pulled pork seasoned with green chili
enchilada sauce cut into easy to handle triangles and finished with
garden tomatoes, sweet sour cream, cheddar cheese and avocado

Sausage Biscuits & Gravy

Light fluffy, melt in your mouth buttermilk seasoned biscuits with a surprise sausage meatball center.
Served hot from the oven with a ladle of satisfying southern sausage gravy

Bacon Chicken Pasta

This savory hearty dish combines tasty egg noodles with tender pulled pieces of chicken breast
and crisp bacon blended in a cheddar herbed cream sauce, oven roasted

Shepherd's Pie

Slowly simmered, onion flavored beef pot roast finished with fresh green beans and a crowning of buttery
whipped potatoes, Asiago cheese and a sprinkling of fresh parsley baked to perfection

Heavenly Chicken Casserole

A hint of Indian curry flavor this heavenly casserole of tender pulled chicken
and broccoli florets tied together with a cheddar cream sauce over earthy wild rice

Chicken Vegetable Stir Fry

Tender chicken breast strips with sweet carrots, garden crisp green beans,
fresh zucchini and red bell pepper tossed in a hot wok adding fluffy scrambled eggs and
sticky fried rice, served steaming hot with a splash of soy sauce

Beef Stroganoff

Flavorful rib eye steak sautéed until tender combined with fragrant onion
and mellow beef gravy over firm and flavorful rigatoni pasta

Chicken Tetrazzini

A taste of home: savory bacon, fresh garden green bell peppers, sweet red onions,
sautéed mushrooms and tender chicken, combined with hearty pasta and
Monterey Jack cheese to make this a dish everyone will enjoy

Karl's Famous Breakfast Burritos ⚜

6 lg. uncooked flour tortillas
2 c. cheddar cheese
¼ c. milk
¼ c. fresh cilantro

1 dozen eggs
1 lb. ground sausage
Hot Sauce

3 oz. can green chilies or jalapeños
½ c. sour cream

Sauté sausage in frying pan until fully cooked. In small bowl beat eggs and milk with wire whisk, pour over sausage and scramble. When eggs are cooked to desired moistness fold in cheese and jalapeños. Cover and keep warm. Over medium heat spread 1 tsp. vegetable oil in a large frying pan. When oil is hot, place 1 large tortilla in pan. Lightly brown both sides of tortilla and set aside in a covered dish keeping warm. Cook all of the tortillas. Spoon egg, cheese and sausage mixture on tortillas. Fold into burrito, top with sour cream and hot sauce. Garnish with fresh cilantro.

Hot Sauce ⚜

6 oz. tomato paste
3 c. water
2 tsp. cayenne pepper

1½ tbsp. chili powder
1 tbsp. minced dried onion
2 tbsp. canned jalapeño slices

2 tsp. white vinegar
2 tsp. cornstarch
2½ tsp. salt

Combine the tomato paste and water in a saucepan over medium heat. Stir until smooth. Add cayenne pepper, chili powder, salt, cornstarch, vinegar and dried onion and stir. Chop jalapeño into fine slices and add to mixture. Bring the mixture to a boil and continue to stir for 3 minutes and remove from heat. Let sauce stand until cool. Place in a tightly sealed container and refrigerate.

Chicken a la King ⚜

4 c. cooked chicken breast

1 c. frozen young peas

1½ tsp. granulated chicken bouillon
    (instead of salt)

6 c. 2% milk

⅔ c. flour

½ c. creamy butter

½ tsp. pepper

Preheat oven to 400°. Place 12 Pepperidge Farms® puff pastry shells in oven and bake for 30 minutes. In 2 qt. pot melt butter, add chicken bouillon and pepper stirring with wire whisk. Fold in flour until all the butter is absorbed. Slightly scorch the roux to deepen flavor. Slowly add milk stirring constantly as sauce thickens. Fold in shredded chicken and frozen peas. When pastry shells are done remove the lid and remove the center of the pastry shell to make room for the sauce. Fill each puff pastry with generous amount of chicken sauce and top with pastry lid. Salt and pepper to taste.

Chicken Rosemary ⚜

4 whole chicken breasts
       boneless, skinless
½ lb. mushrooms
¼ c + 2 tbsp. creamy butter
2½ c. chicken broth
¼ c. flour
1 bottle artichoke hearts (14 oz.)
½ c. aged Parmesan cheese
3 c. wild rice
½ tsp. coarse ground black pepper
¾ c. light cream

2 tbsp. sherry
½ tsp. rosemary
¼ tsp. salt

Cook wild rice according to package instructions and set aside. Take whole chicken breasts and split in half creating 8 sections. Cut each breast half through the thickest part of the breast creating 16 thinner pieces. Lightly tenderize each piece with meat mallet. Slowly simmer chicken pieces in a pot with ½ c. chicken broth until fully cooked. Set aside, saving broth for sauce. Line a buttered 9"x 13" pan (or individual oven safe glassware as pictured) with wild rice, top with chicken pieces. Slice and sauté mushrooms in 2 tbsp. of butter, set aside. In same skillet melt ¼ c. butter adding flour, salt, pepper and rosemary until it forms a roux. Gently fold in cream, sherry and Parmesan cheese . Add in chicken broth and drain the artichoke hearts liquid into sauce. Blend until smooth. Layer artichoke pieces with the chicken in the 9"x 13" pan. Pour sauce over the chicken and top with sautéed mushrooms. Cover with aluminum foil and bake for 30-40 minutes on 325°. (If sauce is too thick add additional chicken broth.)

Pulled Pork Quesadilla

12 lg. flour tortillas
4-6 lbs. pork shoulder roast
1 can green enchilada sauce (19 oz.)
1 tbsp. Worcestershire sauce
¾ c. brown sugar
½ lb. cheddar or Colby Jack cheese
extra virgin olive oil

In a slow cooker cook roast on high for 4 hours or low for 8 hours in two inches of water. Pull pork apart with forks for desired consistency. In a saucepan combine green chili enchilada sauce, Worcestershire sauce and brown sugar. Heat completely until the sugar dissolves and the sauce begins to boil. Pour into slow cooker and combine the pork and sauce completely. In a large skillet heat 1 tsp. of olive oil and lightly fry each side of the uncooked flour tortillas until golden. Cook all tortillas using olive oil as needed. Spread a generous amount of pork on each tortilla. Top with cheese and cover with another freshly cooked tortilla. Keep covered and warm in oven at 200° until ready to serve. Finish with sour cream, cheese and avocado as a garnish.

garnishes:
1 c. sour cream
1 c. cheddar cheese
2 ripe avocados
1 lg. vine ripe tomato

See (pg. 184) Santa Fe Salad (as pictured).

Sausage Biscuits & Gravy ⚜

1½ lbs. spicy ground sausage
1 egg
½ c. oatmeal
1 tsp. dried parsley
¼ c. creamy butter
1 c. buttermilk
3-4 c. milk
1 tsp. garlic salt
½ tsp. onion salt

Preheat oven to 450°. Take 1 lb. of ground sausage, add 1 beaten egg, onion salt and oatmeal. Mix together. Form desired size meatballs. Sauté until lightly brown turning two or three times. Pour ½ c. of water over meatballs and cover, simmer until water is gone and the sausage is fully cooked but moist. Surround each of the sausage balls with the dough and roll in melted butter. Combine garlic salt and dried parsley. Place the buttered biscuits on a cookie sheet and sprinkle with garlic salt and parsley. Bake until golden brown 10-12 minutes. In the same pan cook remaining ½ lb. sausage. Slowly add flour and sauté until golden. Gravy will taste like flour unless you cook it slowly. Add 3-4 c. of milk and let it thicken stirring constantly. Pour over biscuits and enjoy!

Biscuit Dough ⚜

2 c. flour
4 tsp. baking powder
¼ tsp. baking soda
¾ tsp. salt

2 tbsp. creamy butter
2 tbsp. shortening
1 c. buttermilk

Combine flour, baking powder, soda and salt. With a pastry blender cut in butter and shortening creating pea size balls. Add buttermilk and stir to create a soft biscuit dough. Break into individual balls to surround sausage.

Bacon Chicken Pasta ⚜

- 4 whole chicken breasts, boneless, skinless
- 6 slices of bacon
- ½ med. red onion
- 2 tbsp. butter
- 2 tbsp. flour
- 1 tbsp. granulated chicken bouillon
- 12 oz. bag medium egg noodles
- ¾ lb. Monterey Jack cheese, grated
- 1 tsp. fresh gently minced parsley
- ¼ c. water
- ¾ c cream

Preheat oven at 325°. Dice and sauté bacon until crispy. Remove bacon and discard half of the bacon drippings. Dice red onion, sauté in skillet. Quickly add chicken breasts that have been tenderized with a meat mallet and cut into bite size pieces. Sauté on high in skillet turning occasionally. Remove chicken and onion and set aside with bacon. With a wire whisk combine butter, flour and granulated chicken bouillon with bacon drippings and sauté. Slowly fold in cream and water, continue to cook for 2-3 minutes stirring constantly. Cook pasta al dente with salt and olive oil. Drain and rinse pasta. Fold in chicken, onions, ½ of bacon and ½ lb. Jack cheese. Place in 9"x 13" pan (as pictured). Pour sauce over noodle mixture and top with ¼ lb. Jack cheese. Sprinkle top of dish with remaining bacon. Cover with aluminum foil and bake for 45 minutes. Remove aluminum foil and bake for additional 10 minutes until top is crispy. Finish with fresh, gently minced parsley. Serve.

Shepherd's Pie

3-4 lbs. beef pot roast

1 pkg. onion soup mix

2 c. garden green beans

4 brown gravy packets (.87oz. ea.)

1 tbs. extra virgin olive oil

1 tsp. salt

½ tsp. coarse ground pepper

12 lg. garden potatoes

½ c. creamy butter

½-1 c. milk

1 c. Asiago cheese

2 tsp. freshly minced parsley

In a large pot heat oil, salt and pepper until oil pops. Sear roast on all sides to seal moisture and flavor into the roast. Place roast in slow cooker with 4 c. of water and onion soup mix. Slowly cook roast all day or on high for 4 hours. Clean and boil potatoes with 2 tbsp. kosher salt until soft. Drain water and whip potatoes adding butter and milk. Add gravy packets to slow cooker and stir into meat, breaking the roast apart into bite size pieces. Fold in diced green beans, top with mashed potatoes and Asiago cheese. Bake 45 minutes on 375° with lid on. Garnish with freshly minced parsley and serve.

Heavenly Chicken Curry

2 pkg. frozen broccoli florets (10 oz. ea.)

6 chicken breasts cooked, boneless, skinless

2 cans cream of chicken soup (10¾ oz. ea.)

1 c. mayonnaise

1 tbsp. lemon juice

2 tbsp. curry powder

½ c. cheddar cheese

3 boxes Uncle Ben's™ Original Recipe long grain and wild rice (6 oz. ea.)

Preheat oven to 350°. Cook rice according to directions on box and line a 9"x 13" casserole dish or small individual serving dishes (as pictured). In a separate bowl gently pull chicken breasts into bite size pieces. Fold chicken, frozen broccoli, cream of chicken soup, mayonnaise, lemon juice, curry powder and cheddar cheese together, mix gently. Place on top of rice in casserole dish or individual servings and bake at 350° for at least 30 minutes or until bubbly.

Chicken Vegetable Stir Fry ⚜

4 lg. chicken breasts
    boneless, skinless
4 c. sticky rice, uncooked
8 lg. garden carrots
6 sweet green onions
1 ½ c. garden green beans
1 tsp. toasted sesame oil

1 garden zucchini
1 med. red bell pepper
6 eggs
2 tbsp. milk
½ tsp. salt
½ tsp. pepper

Cook rice according to instructions on package. Set aside. Cut chicken breasts in half down the middle. Take each half and slice from side to side into thirds. Place chicken pieces between wax paper, tenderize with meat mallet. Cut chicken into strips and sauté in wok with ½ tsp. toasted sesame oil on high heat. Cut zucchini in fourths, remove seeds and gently cut into small chunks. Clean and cut carrots into bite size pieces, dice green beans, place in wok and drizzle with an additional ½ tsp. toasted sesame oil. Stir fry until vegetables begin to brown on edges. Fold in chopped onions and red bell pepper, continue to cook for 1-2 minutes. Fold in cooked sticky rice and continue to stir fry on high heat. Push rice mix to the side of wok. In a bowl beat six eggs adding milk, salt and pepper and pour in egg mixture. Cook eggs till light and fluffy. When eggs are fully cooked stir into rice and vegetable mix. Add soy sauce to taste.

Beef Stroganoff ⚜

3 rib eye steaks (10 oz. ea.)
3 tbsp. extra virgin olive oil
3 tbsp. granulated beef bouillon
½ c. flour

1 tbsp. dried onion
½ tsp. ground pepper
2 sweet green onion, diced
2 c. sour cream

2 c. 2% milk
2 c. water
12 oz. rigatoni pasta

Generously salt and pepper rib eye steaks. Heat a heavy skillet with 1 tbsp. olive oil and sear rib eye steaks until medium rare or as desired. Remove from skillet and cut into bite size pieces. Sauté 2 tbsp. olive oil and bouillon with rib eye drippings. With a wire whisk fold in flour, dried onion and pepper. Slowly add milk and water to skillet stirring until gravy slightly thickens. Fold in sour cream and rib eye steak pieces. Gravy will be thin with a rich flavor. Cook rigatoni al dente. Rinse and place noodles on plate and top with beef stroganoff. Garnish with diced green onions, salt and pepper to taste.

Chicken Tetrazzini

1½ lbs. chicken tenders
6 slices of bacon
1 lg. sweet red onion
1 lg. green bell pepper
2 c. sliced mushrooms
1 lb. fusilli pasta, dry
1 lb. grated Monterey Jack cheese
2 tsp. fresh chopped chives
½ c. chicken broth
1½ tbsp. granulated chicken bouillon
salt and pepper to taste

Preheat oven to 350°. Spray large stock pot with cooking spray and place chicken tenders in pot. Slowly simmer until chicken is tender. Cut into bite size pieces. In a large sauté pan, cook bacon until crisp. Remove bacon and drain on paper towels but reserve bacon drippings. Chop bacon and set aside. Sauté chopped onions, green pepper and mushrooms with a dash of salt and pepper in reserved bacon drippings. Combine with chicken pieces. Boil fusilli noodles al dente in a large stock pot, adding granulated chicken bouillon to water. When pasta is cooked, rinse in strainer and place in stock pot. Fold in green peppers, red onion, chicken pieces and half of the bacon, toss gently with Monterey Jack cheese. Pour into 9"x13" pan and sprinkle with rest of the bacon and cover with aluminum foil. Bake at 350° for 30 minutes. Remove from oven, add chicken broth and bake for an additional 10 minutes uncovered. Garnish with fresh chives and serve immediately.

❧ Notes & Comments ❧

CHAPTER SEVEN

Savory Beginnings

Sweet Berry Rosemary Flat Bread

Warm herb roasted flat bread spread with a rich, savory blend of cream cheese and plump
mixed berries topped with tender chicken breast sautéed in fresh rosemary

Chicken Wing Fling

Tender wing pieces of chicken lightly fried and coated in a thick, sweet,
and tangy sauce, slowly baked to perfection

Shrimp Ceviche

This island favorite combines citrus marinated shrimp tossed with gently diced sweet onions, vine-ripened
tomatoes, garden green bell peppers and fresh minced cilantro that creates
an appetizing dish served with tortilla chips

Island Salsa

Sweet ripened pineapple, hearty black beans and chopped white onions are combined
to create a fresh island flavor served with tortilla chips

Bacon Tater Tots & Basil Tomato Bites

A crispy grated potato center individually wrapped in savory strips of bacon, served with traditional Italian
flavors of cherry red tomatoes, creamy mozzarella balls and fresh basil leaves

Guacamole Shrimp

Crisp crackers topped with spicy lime guacamole, garnished with sautéed bay shrimp and cilantro

Stuffed Mushrooms

Plump mushrooms filled with a combination of mouth watering bacon, fresh green onions, savory cream cheese and salty potato chips topped with sharp cheddar cheese, oven roasted

Barbecue Chicken Pizza

A perfect compromise of a soft, light, crispy crust topped with a sweet and tangy barbecue sauce, thinly sliced red onions, tender pulled chicken and fresh minced cilantro finished with Monterey Jack cheese

Oven Roasted Sesame Cheese

Toasted sesame seeds coat a blend of savory cream cheese, diced chipped beef and fresh green onions served warm with crackers or our Herb Roasted Flat Bread

Potato Sundae Bar

Tender mashed sweet potatoes, adorned with your choice of oven roasted candied pecans, petite marshmallows lightly dusted with freshly ground nutmeg and sweet brown sugar, being partnered with a generous scoop of baby reds, garnished with your choice of crispy sautéed applewood bacon, crumbled bleu cheese, gently minced fresh basil and chives

Mango Salsa

Fresh mango chunks add special sweetness to a classic favorite to create this unique salsa

Herbed Parmesan Cheese and Oven Roasted Cinnamon Crisps

Oven roasted slender pita chips coated in an aged Parmesan herb blend and sweetened cinnamon for a perfect combination of sweet and salty

Sweet Berry Rosemary Flat Bread ⚜

If bread is made ahead of time, when ready to serve place in aluminum foil and keep warm in 275° oven until ready to serve. Place Sweet Berry Spread in the middle of platter. Surround with Herb Roasted Flat Bread (as pictured.) Garnish with sweet walnuts and Rosemary Chicken. Serve immediately.

Herb Roasted Flat Bread ⚜

2¾ c. flour	1 tbsp. active dry yeast	1 tsp. oregano
1 tsp. salt	1 tbsp. vegetable oil	2 tbsp. extra virgin olive oil
2 tbsp. sugar	1 c. water	1 egg white
1½ c. fresh grated Parmesan	1 tsp. kosher salt	

Preheat oven at 425°. Mix flour, 1 tsp. salt, sugar and yeast. Pour in water and oil and mix with fork. Turn onto a floured surface and knead for 5 minutes until smooth. Brush with olive oil and place in covered bowl for 25 minutes, divide in two sections and roll into round flat bread loaves. Place flat loaves on cookie sheets and brush with olive oil and egg white. Sprinkle with oregano, kosher salt and fresh grated Parmesan. Bake at 425° for 12–15 minutes until crisp.

Rosemary Chicken ⚜

2 chicken breasts
  boneless skinless
2 tbsp. extra virgin olive oil

½ tsp. kosher salt
½ tsp. dried rosemary

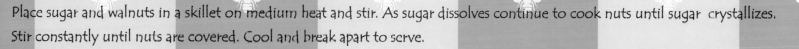

Sauté chicken breast in heavy skillet with olive oil, dried rosemary and kosher salt. Turn chicken two or three times until golden. Slice diagonally just before serving warm.

Sweet Walnuts ⚜

1 c. walnuts
¼ c. sugar

Place sugar and walnuts in a skillet on medium heat and stir. As sugar dissolves continue to cook nuts until sugar crystallizes. Stir constantly until nuts are covered. Cool and break apart to serve.

Sweet Berry Spread ⚜

8 oz. cream cheese
1 c. mixed plump dried fruit
  (Cherries, blueberries raspberries and strawberries)

Blend softened cream cheese with dried plump fruit.

Chicken Wing Fling ⚜

20 chicken wings	1 c. flour	1½ c. sugar
3 eggs	2 tbsp. soy sauce	1 tsp. pepper
1 c. cornstarch	½ c. ketchup	1 tsp. salt
½ c. chicken broth	1 c. vinegar	

Take wings and cut into three pieces, at natural joints. Put tips in a small pot half full of water and simmer to create chicken broth. Remove tips and discard. Beat 2 eggs in small bowl set aside. Blend cornstarch, flour, salt, pepper and mix in a medium size bowl. Dip chicken in egg, flour mix and brown lightly in frying pan. Place side by side in a 9"x 13" pan. Bring to a boil chicken broth (made from tips), soy sauce, ketchup, vinegar and sugar. Pour over chicken, cover half way. Bake at 350° for 90 minutes. Carefully turn chicken pieces every 20 minutes so the sauce has a chance to thicken evenly as the chicken wings bake.

Shrimp Ceviche

1 lb. raw shrimp
7 fresh limes
½ green bell pepper
2 tomatoes
½ white onion
¼ c. minced cilantro
1 tsp. salt
1 tsp. pepper

Wash shrimp and remove skin and tail. Slice in chunks and place in small bowl. Wash limes and slice 6 of them in half. Squeeze the juice of 6 limes over the raw shrimp. Let shrimp soak in lime juice for 25 minutes. The acid in the lime cooks the protein in the shrimp and is ready to eat within a half hour. While the shrimp is soaking, prepare the remaining vegetables. Chop half of one medium sized green bell pepper and two fresh tomatoes into very small chunks. Mince onion and cilantro and combine all vegetables together. When the shrimp has soaked for at least 25 minutes drain lime juice and discard. Add shrimp to the chopped ingredients and toss. Sprinkle salt and pepper and top with the juice of one fresh lime. Refrigerate and serve cold with tortilla chips.

Island Salsa

½ ripe pineapple
½ white onion
1 can black beans (14.5 oz.)
½ tsp. salt

Slice fresh pineapple into small chunks, mince onion and drain canned black beans. Combine all ingredients in small bowl and add salt. Toss and serve cold with tortilla chips.

Bacon Tater Tots™ ⚜

1 lb. bacon (14 slices)   42 frozen Tater Tots™

Preheat oven to 425°. Cut cold bacon in thirds. Wrap a piece of bacon around a frozen Tater Tot™. Secure bacon with toothpick if desired. Spread on large cookie sheet. Bake for 30-40 minutes or until bacon is crisp. Serve immediately.

Basil Tomato Bites ⚜

2 c. cherry tomatoes (1 c. = 25 tomatoes)   12 oz. fresh basil leaves
1 lb. mozzarella cheese   50 toothpicks

Create mozzarella balls by using a melon baller to cut cheese balls. Build Basil Tomato Bites starting with basil, mozzarella ball and tomato (as pictured).

Guacamole Shrimp ⚜

3 ripe avocados

juice of 1 lime

1 tsp. Tabasco™ sauce

½ tsp. cumin

2 tbsp. fresh cilantro

fresh cilantro for garnish

1 lb. shrimp

5 oz. thin crisp crackers

½ tsp. salt

½ tsp. pepper

Mash avocados and add lime juice, Tabasco™ sauce, cumin, salt and pepper. Fold in gently minced cilantro. Lightly sauté shrimp in butter until pink. Place a spoonful of guacamole on cracker, place a sautéed shrimp on top. Garnish with fresh cilantro and serve.

Stuffed Mushrooms ⚜

24 lg. white mushrooms	8 oz. cream cheese	1 c. sharp cheddar cheese
1 lb. bacon	6 mushrooms, minced	salt and pepper to taste
¾ c. crushed potato chips	3 green onions	

Preheat oven to 400°. Dice bacon into small portions and sauté in heavy skillet. When bacon is almost cooked add 6 whole minced mushrooms and 24 minced mushroom stems. Sauté until bacon is crisp. Combine bacon, mushrooms, cream cheese, 2 diced green onions and crushed potato chips in a bowl, mix well. Spoon mixture into hollowed mushrooms. Place mushrooms on cookie sheet, sprinkle with grated cheddar cheese and top with salt and pepper. Bake for 12 minutes. Drain excess liquid from bottom of tray and return to bake for another 8 minutes. Top with diced green onions.

Barbecue Chicken Pizza ⚜

crust:

| 2¼ c. flour | 2 tbsp. sugar | 1 tbsp. oil |
| 1 tsp. salt | 1 tbsp. active dry yeast | 1 c. water |

Preheat oven to 450°. Combine flour, salt, sugar and yeast. Stir together with wire whisk. Add oil and water together and fold into flour mixture with a fork until you form a ball. Turn onto a floured surface and knead for 5-6 minutes until smooth. Brush with olive oil and place in a bowl covered with a damp cloth. Let rise in a warm place 20-25 minutes. When dough has risen, roll out evenly and stretch on a large jelly roll pan, cookie sheet or pizza pan.

toppings:

3 chicken breasts, boneless, skinless	1 tsp. Worcestershire sauce	1 tbsp. extra virgin olive oil
3 c. Monterey Jack cheese	⅛ tsp. black pepper	½ tsp. kosher salt
½ med. red onion	⅓ c. mayonnaise	½ c. Bulls Eye™ Original Barbecue Sauce
⅓ c. cilantro	½ c. ketchup	

As the dough rises, sauté chicken breasts in 1 tbsp. of olive oil and kosher salt on high until tender. Turn 2-3 times, cut into bite size pieces. Whisk together Worcestershire sauce, pepper, mayonnaise, ketchup and barbecue sauce until smooth. Spread the sauce over the entire pizza. Slice the red onion in very thin half rounds. Sprinkle over the sauce, spread chicken evenly over pizza and top with Jack cheese. Finish with fresh minced cilantro. Bake for 15-18 minutes, until completely cooked in the middle. Serve immediately. If prepared as an h'ors d'oeuvre, cook for only 15 minutes. Wrap in aluminum foil and put in 175° oven before serving. Serve right out of the oven.

Oven Roasted Sesame Cheese ⚜

½ c. toasted sesame seeds
1 tbsp. creamy butter
4 oz. cream cheese

¾ c. diced chipped beef
2 green onions

Preheat oven to 425°. Sauté sesame seeds in butter until golden. Set aside. Fold in cream cheese, diced chipped beef and chopped onions together. Mold into a desired shape and roll in toasted seeds. Before serving place in oven for 10 minutes. Serve with your favorite heavy cracker or our Herb Roasted Flat Bread (pg. 150).

Potato Sundae Bar ⚜

baby red mashed potatoes:

> 4 lbs. baby red potatoes
> ½–1 c. milk
> ½ c. creamy butter
> 1 tsp. salt and pepper to taste

Boil potatoes in salted water until tender to the fork. Drain potatoes, add butter and ½ c. milk to potatoes. Whip potatoes adding more milk for desired consistency. Potatoes should be stiffer to form scoop servings. Add salt and pepper to taste. Keep potatoes hot in Sterno™ dish or slow cooker until ready to serve. Serve in individual ice cream sundae cups (as pictured). Garnish with toppings.

mashed sweet potatoes:

    4 lbs. sweet potatoes

    ½–1 c. milk

    ½ c. creamy butter

    salt to taste

Boil sweet potatoes in salted water until tender to the fork. Drain potatoes, add butter and ½ c. milk to potatoes. Whip potatoes adding more milk if desired for consistency. Serve warm.

Oven Roasted Sweet Pecans ⚜

½ c. butter   ¾ c. brown sugar   2 c. pecans

Preheat oven to 375°. Combine melted butter and brown sugar stirring until sugar dissolves. Fold in pecans and spread on a 9"x 13" pan and bake at 375° for 10 minutes. Let cool and break up into pieces.

baby red mashed potato garnishes:

    crumbled bleu cheese

    gently minced basil

    crisp sautéed bacon

    sour cream

sweet mashed potato garnishes:

    oven roasted sweet pecans

    rich brown sugar

    sugared nutmeg dusted marshmallows

    sour cream

Mango Salsa

1 ripe mango
½ med. red onion
½ med. red bell pepper
½ c. cilantro
2 green onions

1 jalapeño
2 tbsp. fresh lime juice
1 tsp. salt
1 clove of garlic
1 tbsp. extra virgin olive oil

Clean and peel ripe mango. Remove pit and dice into small pieces. Mince fresh garlic and jalapeño (with seeds if desired). Dice red bell pepper and green and red onions, chop cilantro and combine all remaining ingredients. Chill before serving. Recipe makes approximately 2 cups salsa.

Herbed Parmesan Crisps ⚜

3 pitas
½ c. creamy butter
1 c. Parmesan cheese
1 tsp. onion salt
2 tsp. parsley flakes

Preheat oven to 375°. Cut pitas in half and slice into thin strips. Pull apart and place in a heavy Ziploc® bag. Melt butter and add to pita strips, shake well. Blend together Parmesan cheese, onion salt and parsley flakes. Pour into Ziploc® bag and coat pita strips evenly. Spread coated strips on a cookie sheet and bake for 12-15 minutes, until crisp. Serve warm or at room temperature. Do not cover or crisps will become soft.

Oven Roasted Cinnamon Crisps ⚜

3 pitas
½ c. creamy butter
2 tsp. cinnamon
1 c. sugar

Preheat oven to 375°. Cut pitas in half and slice into thin strips. Pull apart and place in a heavy Ziploc® bag. Melt butter and add to pita strips and shake well. Blend together cinnamon and sugar. Pour into Ziploc® bag and coat pita strips evenly. Spread coated strips on a cookie sheet and bake for 12-15 minutes, until crisp. Serve warm or at room temperature. Do not cover or crisps will become soft.

CHAPTER EIGHT

Wholesome Soups from the Kitchen

Cream of Mushroom

Fresh mushrooms finely minced and sautéed in butter create a deepened savory base for this creamy soup. Finished with sliced mushrooms and tender green onion stalks

Three Cheese Chicken Tortellini

Torn tender chicken breasts are combined with garden vegetables, blended fresh herbs and dense three cheese tortellini to create this unique soup

French Tomato Soup

The flavors of ripened garden tomatoes, sizzling butter, gently minced fresh basil and a special blend of spices harmonize to complete this savory, creamed soup

Beef Broccoli

Bite-size pieces of rib eye steak, minced onions and mushrooms lightly sautéed in extra virgin olive oil merge with the flavors and textures of sweet tomatoes, broccoli and rice as they combine with a hint of oregano and thyme to form a brothy yet hearty soup

Home Style Chicken Chili

This unique dish blends the classic flavors of chili with sweet corn, flavorful cilantro, tender chicken and savory cream cheese, resulting in a burst of sweet creamy spice. Finished with fresh avocado, ripened garden tomatoes, crisp greens, sour cream and freshly grated cheddar

Potato Bacon Soup

Sautéed baby red potatoes with crisp bacon create a bold flavorful base for this creamy soup, finished with a spicy zest of crushed red chili peppers and garden green onion stalks

Traditional Chili

A new twist on a time honored family recipe will revitalize your palate with the addition of cream cheese, corn and fresh cilantro

Sausage Vegetable Orzo

Italian herbs, savory spicy sausage, sweetened stewed tomatoes, crisp garden carrots and tender green onion stalks combine to create this hearty blend

Chicken Stir Fry Soup

Crispy stir fry vegetables gently sautéed in hot sesame oil combined with pulled chicken are added to a steaming bowl of chicken broth to create this appetizing dish

Ginger Beef Soup

Seared and slowly cooked pot roast infused with the flavors of tender green onions, large garden carrots, fresh green beans, minced fresh ginger and bay leaves, as these flavorful ingredients are combined with acini di pepe pasta and baby red potatoes to create this filling meal

Chicken Barley

Pearl barley and savory chicken are combined with garden fresh vegetables, fused with savory spices to create this healthy, low-calorie dish that will leave every appetite satisfied.

Cream of Mushroom

¾ c. creamy butter

4 c. sliced mushrooms

1-1¼ c. flour

2 tbsp. granulated chicken bouillon

8 c. 2% milk

1 pt. heavy cream

4 fresh green onions

½ tsp. coarse ground pepper

Take 1 c. of sliced mushrooms and set aside. In a large soup pot melt ¼ c. of butter, dice 3 c. of mushrooms and sauté until mushrooms darken in color. Add remaining ½ c. of butter, fold in flour, pepper and bouillon, creating a roux. Scorch the roux to deepen the flavor stirring constantly on medium heat. Slowly fold in with a whisk the cream and milk to desired consistency. Soup will thicken as it cooks. To thin down soup fold in more milk. Add half of the diced green onions. In a separate pan sauté 1 c. of sliced mushrooms to use as a garnish. When ready to serve, top with sautéed mushroom slices and diced green onions. *Helpful Hint: To reheat soup make sure not to bring to a boil or the soup will separate.*

Three Cheese Chicken Tortellini ⚜

20 oz. pkg. fresh three cheese tortellini

8 c. water

4 tbsp. granulated chicken bouillon

4 cooked chicken breasts
   boneless, skinless

6 lg. garden carrots

4 stalks of celery

¼ med. red bell pepper

6 garden green onions

½ c. freshly minced basil

Cook three cheese tortellini al dente. In a large stock pot combine water, chicken bouillon, chopped celery and carrots. Simmer for 5- 10 minutes. Add cooked torn chicken breasts, diced red bell pepper and tortellini. Fold in green onions and gently minced fresh basil, heat completely. Salt and pepper to taste. Serve immediately.

French Tomato Soup ⚜

8 ripe tomatoes
2 tbsp. creamy butter
1 med. onion
2 cloves garlic
1 tsp. Maggi™
1 tsp. Accent™

1 tbsp. paprika
3 tbsp. flour
2 tbsp chicken granulated bouillon
2 tbsp. parsley (4 tbsp. fresh)
1 tbsp. sweet basil (3 tbsp. fresh)
2 c. water

2 c. heavy cream
1/8 tsp. grated nutmeg
1/4 c. minced cilantro
1 tsp. salt
1/4 c. sugar
1 tsp. dry mustard

Scald and peel tomatoes, set aside. Melt butter in large saucepan and sauté chopped onions, add minced garlic and continue to sauté. Add Maggi™, Accent™, dry mustard, paprika, flour, chicken base, parsley and basil. Cut up tomatoes and add to saucepan with 2 c. water. Bring to a boil and simmer 15-20 minutes until tomatoes collapse. Put in blender and purée until smooth. Return to pan. (Can be put in freezer bags or containers at this point and frozen.) Gradually add 2 c. heavy cream, half and half or milk. Add 1/8 teaspoon grated nutmeg. Add salt and sugar. Bring just to a boil and stir with a whisk. Garnish with cilantro and serve warm.

Beef Broccoli ⚜

2 rib eye steaks (10 oz. ea.)	1 can tomato sauce (8 oz.)	2 tbsp. granulated beef bouillon
1 med. yellow onion	1 tbsp. sugar	8 c. water
2 c. mushrooms	1 tsp. oregano	2 tbsp. extra virgin olive oil
2 c. fresh broccoli	1 tsp. thyme	1 tsp. coarse ground black pepper
1½ c. rice, uncooked	1 tsp. salt	

Cut rib eye steaks into bite size pieces. Lightly salt and pepper and sauté in hot olive oil until tender. Add sliced mushrooms and chopped onions. Continue to sauté adding oregano, thyme, pepper, sugar and beef bouillon. Fold in tomato sauce and simmer for 5 minutes. Add rice and water and cook for 25 minutes. Add broccoli and simmer for 5 minutes. (Do not over cook or broccoli will be too soft.)

Home Style Chicken Chili ⚜

3 lbs. chicken tenders

2 lg. cans tomato sauce (29 oz. ea.)

1 lg. can crushed tomato (29 oz.)

1 bag frozen corn (16 oz.)

2 c. fresh green beans

3 cans kidney beans (15 oz. ea.)

2 cans black beans (15 oz. ea.)

4 tbsp. hot chili powder

4 tbsp. cumin

4 tbsp. oregano

8 oz. cream cheese

1 c. fresh cilantro

½ c. sugar

salt and pepper to taste

Place frozen chicken tenders in a large pot that has been sprayed with cooking spray. Lightly salt and pepper chicken tenders. Cover, allow chicken to cook until tender for 10-12 minutes. When chicken is completely cooked, using forks, pull apart into bite-size pieces and return to pot. Add all other ingredients and 1 c. of water. Simmer for an hour. As a garnish prepare chopped fresh tomatoes, dice avocados, grated cheese, torn lettuce and gently minced fresh cilantro. Finish with sour cream and your favorite tortilla chips.

Potato Bacon Soup ⚜

2 lbs. bacon

20 sm. baby red potatoes

½–1 c. flour

4 green onions

½ tsp. crushed red chili peppers

3 tbsp. granulated chicken bouillon

2 c. cream

2 qts. milk

fresh ground pepper to taste

Dice bacon and sauté in deep pot until crisp. Remove cooked bacon bits and set aside. Cut baby red potatoes into chunks and fry in bacon drippings until crisp around edges. Remove potatoes from drippings and set aside. Add enough flour to remaining bacon drippings so the liquid is completely absorbed. Stir in chicken bouillon, crushed red chilies and sauté for 3–4 minutes until roux darkens in color. Continue stirring, slowly adding the cream. As sauce thickens, add 1 quart milk. Fold in diced green onions, bacon and potatoes. Add remaining milk until desired thickness is achieved. Top with fresh ground pepper to taste. *Helpful Hint: Sauce thickens over time so additional milk may be necessary for desired thickness when reheated.*

Traditional Chili ⚜

3 lbs. ground beef

3 green onions

1 med. yellow onion

4 tbsp. hot chili powder

4 tbsp. cumin

4 tbsp. oregano

2 tbsp. Worcestershire sauce

¾ c sugar

2 cans stewed tomatoes (14.5 oz. ea.)

2 lg. cans tomato sauce (29 oz. ea.)

8 oz. cream cheese

1½ c. white corn

2 lg. cans kidney beans (40 oz. ea.)

2 c. shredded sharp cheese

1 c. diced cilantro

In a large stock pot sauté ground beef and minced green and yellow onions. When meat is fully cooked, add chili powder, cumin, oregano and Worcestershire sauce. Fold in sugar, stewed tomatoes, tomato sauce, cream cheese and corn. Add drained kidney beans and simmer for an hour. Serve chili topped with sharp cheese and diced cilantro.

Sausage Vegetable Orzo

2 lbs. spicy ground sausage

10 oz. package of orzo pasta

2 cans Italian style stewed tomatoes (14.5 oz. ea.)

2 tbsp. sugar

½ tsp. oregano

6 c. chicken broth

4 lg. carrots

3 garden green onions

½ c. freshly minced basil

In a large soup pot sauté sausage, drain drippings and return sausage to pot. Add orzo to pot and sauté. Stir in stewed tomatoes, sugar, oregano and chicken broth. Simmer for 30 minutes. Peel and cut carrots into thick chunks. Add to orzo soup and simmer for 15 minutes. Do not over cook, keep vegetables crisp. Fold in fresh basil, chopped green onions and serve.

Chicken Stir Fry Soup ⚜

4 chicken breasts, boneless, skinless

6 lg. carrots

2 c. chopped broccoli

2 c. snow peas

1 med. red bell pepper

1 med. yellow bell pepper

1 sm. sweet yellow onion

1 tbsp. hot sesame oil

6 c. chicken broth

Tenderize chicken with a meat mallet and slice in chunks. Chop onion, peel and cut carrots in medium size pieces, slice red and yellow bell peppers and chop broccoli. In wok, heat sesame oil on high. Add chicken and stir fry. Combine all vegetables in wok and stir fry for 3-4 minutes. Fold in snow peas. Cook an additional minute. Add chicken broth, bring to a boil, do not over cook. Serve immediately.

Ginger Beef Soup ⚜

4 lbs. beef pot roast

2 tbsp. extra virgin olive oil

1 fresh bay leaf

¹/₃ c. chives

2 c. garden fresh green beans

20 baby red potatoes

4 tender green onions

1 tsp. pepper

8 lg. garden carrots

2 tsp. ginger, freshly minced

3 tbsp. beef bouillon

2 pkg. Lipton™ onion soup mix

1 tsp. salt

1 lb. Acini di pepe pasta
(tiny round pasta, larger than couscous)

Sear pot roast in a large pot on stove with olive oil, salt and pepper. Cook roast on high until browned on all sides. Add enough water to cover meat. Add one fresh bay leaf, two packages onion soup mix and chives. Simmer on low 4–6 hours or use a slow cooker. When meat is tender and falls apart easily, cut into large portions. Chop carrots and potatoes into chunks, combine fresh green beans, beef bouillon and fresh minced ginger, add to meat. Let simmer for 15–20 minutes (be careful not to over cook vegetables). Add additional water to taste if needed. Prepare pasta according to directions on package substituting chicken bouillon for salt. Strain pasta and set aside. When serving, separately place a half cup of pasta in bowl along with Ginger Beef Soup (as pictured). Top with gently diced green onions.

Chicken Barley ⚜

4 chicken breasts, boneless, skinless
¾ c. pearl barley
3 stalks of celery
3 carrots
2 lg. tomatoes

2 cloves fresh garlic
2 tbsp. soy sauce
2 tbsp. fresh minced basil
4 tbsp. granulated chicken bouillon
8 c. water

4 garden green onions
½ tsp. oregano
½ tsp. thyme
dash cayenne pepper
2 tbsp. chopped fresh parsley

In large soup pot place water, chicken breasts, pearl barley, chopped celery and carrots, diced tomatoes, fresh minced cloves of garlic, soy sauce, basil, chicken bouillon, oregano, thyme and dash of cayenne pepper. Bring to a boil and simmer for 1½ hours. Remove chicken breasts and tear into bite size pieces. Fold back into the soup and add fresh parsley and diced garden green onions. Serve.

❦ Notes & Comments ❦

CHAPTER NINE

⚜ Garden Fresh Salads ⚜

Waldorf Chicken Salad

Fresh spring mixed greens, tender grilled chicken breast, sweet red grapes, crisp tart apples and toasted candied walnuts topped with a Sweet Onion Dijon Dressing

Tortellini Turkey Salad

A delicious mix of hearty three cheese tortellini, fresh oven roasted turkey, sweet honey baked ham, spicy cured salami, freshly minced basil, crisp bell peppers, sweet yellow corn and black beans tossed together with Gorgonzola Ranch Dressing

Oriental Chicken Salad

This classic favorite is filled with crunch! The combination of chilled, grilled chicken breast, roasted almonds, crunchy ramen noodles, toasted sesame seeds, shredded Napa cabbage finished with a Sweet Sesame Dressing is flavorful in every bite

Barbecue Chicken Salad

Tender sweetened barbecue chicken tossed with fresh mixed greens, garden ripe tomatoes, sweet young corn, black beans and freshly grated Jack cheese, topped with a tangy ranch dressing

Chicken Wonton Salad

Tender sautéed chicken strips, crispy golden wontons, shredded Napa cabbage, julienned vegetables, folded together and finished with a sweet Peanut Ginger Dressing

Spring Mix Fruit Salad

Candied walnuts, chopped celery, seedless red grapes, chunks of Granny Smith apples, crumbly aged Gorgonzola cheese on a bed of spring mixed greens finished with a Sweet Balsamic Dressing

Santa Fe Salad

A medley of red, yellow and green bell peppers, hearty black beans, sweet yellow corn, ripe avocado, garden fresh tomatoes, Monterey Jack cheese and savory smoked bacon tossed with a sweet cilantro dressing

Turkey Penne Salad

This refreshing mix of pasta and greens is filled with an assortment of bell peppers, English cucumbers, tender sugar snap peas, freshly roasted turkey breast tossed with a Zesty Lime Dressing

Spring Shrimp Salad

A combination of garden green cucumbers, fresh bay shrimp, hearty shell pasta and tender hearts of romaine lettuce finished with a Sweet Onion Dressing

Bacon Potato Salad

A simple yet satisfying blend of baby red potatoes and crisp savory bacon, covered in a light but rich Creamy Cilantro Dressing

Waldorf Chicken Salad ⚜

12 oz. spring mix greens
2 med. heads hearts of romaine lettuce
4 grilled chicken breasts, torn

1 Pink Lady apple
2 lg. Granny Smith apples
2 c. seedless grapes

1½ c. candied walnuts
2 c. diced celery
Sweet Onion Dijon Dressing

Clean and tear hearts of lettuce. Toss with spring mix, add grapes, diced apples and celery to lettuce. Fold in Candied Walnuts and torn chicken. Toss with Sweet Onion Dijon Dressing to taste just before serving.

Candied Walnuts ⚜

1½ c. chopped walnuts   ¼ c. + 1 tbsp. sugar   1 tbsp. water

Place chopped walnuts in skillet on high, heat and sprinkle ¼ c. sugar over the top and stir. As it heats, pour 1 tbsp. water evenly over nuts and stir to evenly coat. Add one more tbsp. sugar and stir, turn off heat. Cool nuts and set aside for salad.

Sweet Onion Dijon Dressing ⚜

3 tbsp. Dijon mustard
1 c. sugar
2 tbsp. dried onion
1 tsp salt
⅔ c red wine vinegar
½ c. water
1½ c. vegetable oil

Mix together in blender. Chill.

Tortellini Turkey Salad ⚜

20 oz. three cheese tortellini

10 oz. spring mix greens

4 tbsp. fresh basil, gently minced

½ lb. oven roasted deli turkey

½ lb. honey baked ham

¼ lb. spicy cured salami

1 bag frozen corn (12 oz.)

1 lg. red bell pepper

½ lg. orange bell pepper

½ lg. yellow bell pepper

15 oz. can black beans

Cook tortellini al dente and chill. Slice spicy salami into long strips, dice bell peppers, cut honey baked ham and oven roasted turkey into chunks. Gently mince fresh basil, rinse black beans and toss with frozen corn and spring mix. Place all ingredients in serving bowl and pour half of the Gorgonzola Ranch Dressing over top. Add more to taste. Toss salad and serve.

Gorgonzola Ranch Dressing ⚜

1 c. milk

1 c. mayonnaise

1 tbsp. white vinegar or lemon juice

1 tbsp. ranch mix (pg. 188)

1 c. crumbled Gorgonzola cheese

Add white vinegar or lemon juice to milk. Combine mayonnaise, milk and ranch mix with wire whisk and fold in Gorgonzola cheese. Refrigerate.

Oriental Chicken Salad ⚜

½ c. roasted slivered almonds

¼ c. creamy butter

1 pkg. chicken ramen noodle soup mix

½ c. sesame seeds

1 head Napa cabbage

6 green onions

4 chicken breasts, cooked

Sweet Sesame Dressing

Preheat oven to 325°. Place almonds on cookie sheet and roast in oven for 10 minutes. Sauté butter and crumbled ramen noodles, seasoning packet and sesame seeds in a skillet until brown. This will deepen the flavor. Allow to cool to room temperature. Before serving, shred Napa cabbage, dice onions and pull chicken breasts into large bite size pieces. Toss with noodle mixture and roasted almonds. Top with Sweet Sesame Dressing to taste. Serve immediately.

Sweet Sesame Dressing ⚜

½ c. vegetable oil

1 tsp. sesame oil

1½ tsp. soy sauce

½ c. sugar

¼ c. rice or white vinegar

½ tsp. salt

½ tsp. ground pepper

Mix dressing ingredients, chill.

Barbecue Chicken Salad ⚜

2 heads hearts of romaine lettuce

2 c. Monterey Jack cheese

1 c. frozen young white corn

1 c. black beans

4 green onions

2 ripe tomatoes

2 c. tortilla strips

3 c. chopped barbecue chicken

Clean and shred lettuce. Chill. Dice tomatoes and onions, set aside. Combine frozen corn and black beans. Fold in Jack cheese and toss with lettuce, diced tomatoes and onions. Top with barbecue chicken and tortilla strips. Finish with Spicy Salsa Ranch (pg. 12) to taste just before serving.

Barbecue Chicken Sauce ⚜

½ tsp. Worcestershire sauce

3 tbsp. mayonnaise

3 c. chopped cooked chicken

¼ c. ketchup

¼ c. barbecue sauce

Mix together Worcestershire sauce, mayonnaise, ketchup and barbecue sauce, fold in chopped chicken, chill.

Chicken Wonton Salad ⚜

1 large head Napa cabbage

2 lg. carrots

1 head hearts of romaine lettuce

1 pkg. wonton wrappers

6 chicken breasts, boneless, skinless

3 c. vegetable oil

4 green onions

1 tbsp. extra virgin olive oil

1 c. roasted peanuts (optional)

1 tsp. sea salt

½ tsp. ground black peppercorn

Cut chicken breasts in half down the middle, taking each half and slicing across from side to side into thirds. Placing chicken pieces between wax paper, tenderize with meat mallet. In a heavy skillet on high, heat oil and salt. Place chicken breast pieces in hot oil and sauté, turning twice until golden. Remove from pan and cut into thin strips, set aside. Heat on high 3 c. oil in a large stock pot. Slice wontons in thin strips and fry until golden. Clean and shred Napa cabbage and hearts of romaine lettuce. Chill. Clean and peel carrots, grate. Dice green onion and combine with cabbage, lettuce and carrots. Just before serving fold together with wontons and chicken. Top with Peanut Ginger Dressing to taste and serve.

Peanut Ginger Dressing ⚜

¼ c. rice vinegar

3 tbsp. fresh minced ginger

¾ c. peanut butter

½ c. sugar

¼ c. white vinegar

¼ c. soy sauce

½ tsp. pepper

3 oz. frozen orange juice concentrate

Place all ingredients in blender and puree. Chill.

Spring Mix Fruit Salad ⚜

2 c. candied walnuts

12 oz. crumbled Gorgonzola Cheese

20 oz. Spring Mix

2 c. seedless red grapes

2 stalks of celery

2 Granny Smith apples

Clean and cut grapes in half, core and cut apples in bite size pieces. Dice celery and combine with spring mix. Before serving toss with grapes, walnuts and Gorgonzola cheese. Top with Sweet Balsamic dressing to taste.

Candied Walnuts ⚜

1½ c. chopped walnuts

¼ c. + 1 tbsp. sugar

1 tbsp. water

Place chopped walnuts in skillet on high heat and sprinkle ¼ c. sugar over the top. Stir. As it heats, pour 1 tbsp. water evenly over nuts and stir to evenly coat. Add one more tbsp. sugar and stir. Turn off heat. Cool nuts and set aside for salad.

Sweet Balsamic ⚜

½ c. sugar

¼ c. balsamic vinegar

⅓ med. red onion

3 cloves garlic

⅓ c. rice vinegar

½ tsp. salt

¼ tsp. pepper

juice of 1 lime

¼ c. Parmesan cheese

2 tbsp. sour cream

½ c. vegetable oil

Mix together in blender and chill.

Santa Fe Salad ⚜

2 heads hearts of romaine lettuce

2 c. black beans

1 c. diced tomatoes

½ med. red bell pepper

½ med. yellow bell pepper

½ med. green bell pepper

1 c. corn

2 ripe avocados

8 slices smoked bacon

1 c. shredded Monterey Jack cheese

Sauté bacon slices until crisp, break into small pieces. Clean and shred hearts of romaine, drain and rinse black beans, chop avocado, dice tomato and peppers. Before serving toss together all ingredients adding bacon, corn and shredded Jack cheese. Top with Sweet Jalapeño Cilantro Dressing to taste.

Sweet Jalapeño Cilantro Dressing ⚜

3 jalapeño peppers, seeded except for one

1 c. vegetable oil

⅓ c. sugar

½ c. white wine vinegar

1 tsp. salt

2 tbsp. mayonnaise

½ c. fresh cilantro

In blender or food processor puree the jalapeños (leave seeds in according to desired taste) with oil, vinegar, sugar and salt. Continue processing and add mayonnaise, blending until emulsified. Add cilantro and blend until finely chopped.

Turkey Penne Salad ⚜

1 lb. hearty penne pasta
1 med. red bell pepper
1 med. yellow bell pepper

1 English cucumber
2 c. sugar snap peas

3 c. diced deli turkey breast
1 head hearts of romaine lettuce

Cook pasta al dente. Cut sugar snap peas in half, dice English cucumber and red and yellow peppers. Clean and tear lettuce. Combine diced turkey, cooked pasta, bell peppers, cucumber and snap peas. Toss with Zesty Lime Dressing to taste just before serving.

Zesty Lime Dressing ⚜

½ med. sweet red onion
juice of 2 limes (¼ c.)
¾ c. sugar

½ c. oil
½ c. rice vinegar

½ tsp. salt
½ tsp. freshly ground peppercorn

Mix together in a blender, Chill.

Spring Shrimp Salad ⚜

1 head hearts of romaine lettuce	2 lbs. bay shrimp	2 tsp. extra virgin olive oil
1 English cucumber	12 oz. shell pasta	1 tsp. salt

Cook pasta al dente using olive oil and salt added to water. Drain and rinse, Chill. Clean and cut heart of romaine lettuce into bite size pieces. Dice English cucumber and toss with lettuce, Chill. Rinse shrimp and combine with pasta, lettuce and English cucumber. Finish with Sweet Onion Dressing to taste.

Sweet Onion Dressing ⚜

½ med. red onion	½ c. rice vinegar	½ c. honey
1 tbsp. dried green onion	½ tsp. onion salt	⅓ c. sugar
½ c. vegetable oil	½ tsp. pepper	½ tsp. black sesame seeds

Mix together in blender all ingredients except sesame seed, chill. Garnish with black sesame seeds.

Bacon Potato Salad ⚜

4 lbs. baby red potatoes   2 lbs. bacon

Clean and pierce red potatoes. Place in pot and cover with hot water and 2 tsp. kosher salt. Bring to a boil and cook until potatoes are tender but firm. Drain potatoes and rinse. Slice in half for bite size servings. Chill. Sauté diced bacon until crisp. Set aside 2 tsp. bacon drippings for dressing. Combine sliced potatoes and bacon in a bowl and drizzle with Creamy Cilantro Dressing to taste. Chill before serving.

Creamy Cilantro Dressing ⚜

⅓ c. mayonnaise   2 tsp. bacon drippings   ½ c. minced cilantro
4 tbsp. sugar   ⅓ c. white wine vinegar

In a blender combine all ingredients and mix well. Chill. Shake well before serving.

Homemade Dry Ranch Dressing Mix

20 saltines
2 c. dry minced parsley flakes
½ c. dry minced onion
2 tbsp. dry dill weed
¼ c. onion salt
¼ c. garlic salt
¼ c. garlic powder
¼ c. onion powder

Put crackers through blender on high speed until powdered. Add parsley, minced onions and dill weed. Blend again until powdered. Dump into bowl. Stir in onion salt, garlic salt, onion powder and garlic powder. Put into container with tight fitting lid. Store dry mix at room temperature for up to a year.

Homemade Ranch Dressing

1 tbsp. Dry Ranch Mix
1 c. mayonnaise
1 c. milk
1 tbsp. white vinegar or lemon juice

Combine milk and white vinegar or lemon juice. Fold in mayonnaise and Dry Ranch Mix. Keep refrigerated.

Notes & Comments

CHAPTER TEN

⚜ *Enchanting Desserts* ⚜

Oreo™ Chocolate Banana Cream Pie

Five luscious layers of sweet delight beginning with a chocolaty crust of crushed Oreos™
covered in smooth white chocolate, fresh sliced bananas, filled with a light creamy
vanilla pudding, topped with dollops of fresh whipped cream

Star Cookie Crunch

Superstar cookies! A decadent chewy devil's food brownie smoothed with melted milk chocolate, topped
with a crispy blend of light crunchy peanut butter cut into super stars.

Mini Carrot Bundt Cake

Mouth watering, moist, seductively spiced, fresh shredded carrot cake drizzled with
a velvety vanilla cream cheese glaze

Butter Tarts

A traditional family favorite of glazed sweet plump raisins and earthy pecans in
delicious flaky pastry tarts

Chocolate Crisp Cupcake

Amazing! Marshmallow chocolate crisp cups rimmed with silky chocolate and filled with
fresh summer strawberries in sweetened whipped cream. Top with sliced strawberries

Blueberry Torte

Dazzling, delicious blueberry pie filling on a cloud of sweet whipped cream cheese,
crusted in minced sugared pecans

Chocolate Covered Strawberries

A beautiful and delicious gourmet treat. Large, luscious fresh ripe strawberries dipped in sweet smooth milk and dark chocolate, drizzled with contrasting mellow chocolate

Fabulous Fudge

Rich, thick, creamy, delightful, semi-sweet chocolate fudge squares topped with a tasty roasted pecan

Coconut Cake

Party Pretty! Three tiers of rich coconut cake sandwiched between layers of vanilla infused buttercream frosting and finished with fluffy white shredded coconut

Coffee Pound Cream Cake

Supple, creamy pound cake with a hint of aromatic nutmeg topped with soulful cinnamon, brown sugar crumbles and drizzled with a lush almond flavored icing

Cream Cheese Brownies

Rich, delicious, decadent chocolate swirled with soft cream cheese for melt in your mouth delight

Raspberry Truffles

Silky smooth chocolate ganache candies blended with a taste of fragrant raspberries rolled and finished in a sweet cocoa powder

Peanut Butter Balls

Simply delightful, smooth creamy peanut butter balls with an unexpected crispy crunch
coated in sweet chocolate candy coating

Blueberry Coffee Cake

Moist golden yellow cake baked with tender fresh flavorful blueberries, generously topped
with buttery cinnamon sugar crumbles. Served warm with whipped cream
or natural vanilla bean ice cream

Pumpkin Mousse

Relive the flavors of fall anytime with this light creamy mousse of sweet pumpkin, freshly ground nutmeg
and fragrant pumpkin pie spices alternately layered with fresh whipped cream and
gently crushed Orange Ginger Snap Cookies, crowned with a dollop of whipped cream

Orange Ginger Snap Cookies

Ground ginger, finely grated orange rind and sweet molasses enhance the homespun
goodness of these crisp orange sugar coated cookies

Raspberry Cheese Cake

A seductive layer of pink raspberry cream cheese frozen atop lemony cream cheese filling, in a bed of
crushed graham crackers. Top this frozen treat with a sprinkle of whole raspberries

Coconut Balls

Silky smooth chocolate cream truffles blended with fresh flaky coconut, rolled in
more of the sweet white flakes

Crispy Peanut Butter Squares

Peanut butter Rice Krispie™ squares topped with creamy milk chocolate ready in under five minutes. A great after school treat or last minute dessert

Coconut Chex™ Mix

Compatible flavors unite in this crunchy mix of sweet Golden Grahams™, toasted slivered almonds, crisp Corn Chex™ and shredded coconut in a shiny sugar glaze

Chocolate Almond Chex™ Mix

A memorable mix of mellow white chocolate chips, savory almonds, crunchy Corn Chex™, shredded coconut and lightly sweet Golden Grahams™ in a clear sugar coating

Butter Crisp Cookies

These oatmeal inspired cookies are sweet, crisp, buttery rolled oats, dipped in a delicious creamy chocolate coating

Peanut Butter Bars

Old fashioned goodness. Nutty peanut butter and rolled oat bars frosted with melted peanut butter and dark chocolate morsels

Banana Cream Pie

A sensational finale to any meal. Tender flaky pie crust lined with delicious ripe banana slices, topped with whipped cream, vanilla pudding and finished with a dollop or two of fresh dreamy whipped cream

Oreo™ Chocolate Banana Cream Pie ⚜

20 Oreo™ double stuffed™ cookies

2 tbsp. creamy butter

8 oz. white chocolate chips

4 lg. bananas

2 c. milk

1 lg. box vanilla instant pudding mix (5.1 oz.)

½ c. sugar

2 c. whipping cream

2 tsp. vanilla

2 oz. grated milk chocolate bar

Remove the frosting from 20 Oreo™ cookies, set aside. Using a rolling pin, crush all of the cookies in a heavy Ziploc® bag. Combine cookie frosting and butter in bowl and place in microwave for 30 seconds. Blend with crushed cookies and press cookie mixture into a pie tin or deep fluted loose base tart pan (as pictured). Melt white chocolate chips. Spread a thin layer of melted chocolate over crust, placing a thicker portion of the white chocolate on the upper edge so it is visible when displayed. Place in freezer for 5 minutes. Blend together pudding mix and 2 c. of milk using a whisk, mix well. Beat whipping cream in a chilled bowl on high until stiff peaks appear. Fold in vanilla and sugar blend until creamy. Fold 2 c. whipped cream into pudding, mix well. Slice bananas and place on the bottom of the pie crust. Fill the pie with the pudding mixture. Top with remaining 1 c. of whipped cream. Sprinkle grated chocolate bar for garnish. Refrigerate before serving.

Star Cookie Crunch

1 devils food cake mix
½ c. peanut butter
2 eggs

½ c. sugar
½ c. vegetable oil
½ c. Karo™ syrup

8 oz. white chocolate chips
4 c. Rice Krispies™
8 oz. semi-sweet chocolate chips

Preheat oven to 350°. These cookies are made in two layers. Blend cake mix with eggs and vegetable oil. Fold in white chocolate chips. Press cookie dough into a 9"x13" baking pan and bake for 10 minutes. While dough is baking, melt Karo™ syrup, peanut butter and sugar in a heavy 2 qt. saucepan. Stir over medium heat, until smooth and remove from heat. Fold in Rice Krispies™ until evenly coated. Heat semi-sweet chips in microwave for 1-1½ minutes stirring every 30 seconds until smooth. Spread evenly over baked cookie layer. Spread Rice Krispies™ mixture over warm semi-sweet chocolate and press firmly. As the chocolate cools, the Rice Krispies™ will stick to the brownie cookie layer. Before completely cooled, cut the cookies with star shaped cookie cutters and chill.

Mini Carrot Bundt Cake ⚜

1 c. flour

1 c. sugar

1 tsp. soda

1 tsp. cinnamon

¼ tsp. salt

¼ tsp. allspice

¾ c. + 2 tbsp. vegetable oil

2 eggs

1½ c. grated carrots

Preheat oven to 350°. Mix together flour, sugar, soda, cinnamon, salt and allspice in a bowl. Add vegetable oil, beaten eggs and grated carrots. Mix on medium speed for 2 minutes. Pour into a mini bundt pan or an 8" round cake pan. Bake at 350° for 20-25 minutes or until toothpick comes out clean. Remove from bundt pan and place on cake stand. Frost warm cake with cream cheese icing to form a glaze. (To make in a regular bundt cake pan simply double the recipe.)

Cream Cheese Frosting ⚜

4 oz. cream cheese

¼ c. butter

2 tsp. vanilla

6 tbsp. milk

3-4 c. powdered sugar

Mix ingredients together until smooth and frost on warm cake.

Butter Tarts ⚜

filling:

- ¼ c. creamy butter
- ½ c. brown sugar
- 1 c. corn syrup
- 2 eggs
- 1 tsp. lemon juice
- 1 c. plump raisins
- ½ c. gently chopped pecans (optional)
- 1 tsp. rich vanilla

Preheat oven to 375°. Make pastry. To prevent butter tarts from bubbling over, stir as little as possible. Pour boiling water over raisins. Let stand 5 minutes and drain. Stir together melted butter, brown sugar and corn syrup. Lightly beat 2 eggs and fold into butter sauce, adding vanilla, lemon juice, raisins and pecans. Fill pastry-lined tarts evenly with filling. (Be careful not to drip on the edges, it will cause pastry to stick and make it difficult to remove tarts.) Bake for 15-20 minutes, or until pastry is golden.

Pastry ⚜

- 2 c. flour
- 1 tsp. salt
- ¾ c. shortening
- 6-7 tbsp. ice water

Sift flour and salt together, cut in shortening with pastry blender until pieces are the size of small peas. Sprinkle ice water over dough. Gently mix forming two medium size balls of pastry. Turn onto a floured surface, handling as little as possible. Roll out pastry. Use a quart jar to cut circles of pastry to line regular size muffin tray. Do not prick pastry. Makes 20-24 tarts.

Chocolate Crisp Cupcakes ⚜

²/₃ c. creamy butter

1 lb. bag marshmallows

7 c. Cocoa Krispies™

2 c. sliced strawberries

2 c. whipping cream

¹/₃–¹/₂ c. sugar

1 tsp. rich vanilla

²/₃ c. semi-sweet chocolate chips

In a large pot melt butter and marshmallows on low. Melt marshmallows until creamy, be careful not to cook. Fold in Cocoa Krispies™. Spray deep popover trays with cooking spray and fill with Cocoa Krispies™ mixture forming a shell with a hollow center. Place in fridge to cool and set up. Melt chocolate chips in microwave, stirring every 30 seconds until smooth. Dip cocoa cups in melted chocolate just on the top edges (as pictured). Whip cream on high until stiff. Beat in sugar and vanilla to taste. Fold in sliced strawberries, Fill cocoa cups with strawberry cream filling, top with fresh strawberry slice. Chill. When ready to serve, let sit for 5 minutes. The crispy cups will soften and be easy to cut when eating.

Blueberry Torte ⚜

crust:

⅓ c. brown sugar	1 c. flour	½ c. creamy butter	1 c. gently chopped pecans

Preheat oven to 350°. In a large bowl, mix brown sugar and flour. Cut in butter and chopped pecans. Press into a greased 10" springform pan. Bake for 20 minutes. Cool in refrigerator.

filling:

1⅓ c. sugar	1½ c. Cool Whip™
12 oz. softened cream cheese	1 can blueberry pie filling (21 oz.)

Whip cream cheese and sugar together, fold in Cool Whip™. Spread filling into cooled crust. Top with blueberry pie filling and chill.

Chocolate Dipped Strawberries ⚜

6 oz. semi-sweet chocolate chips
10 oz. milk chocolate chips
½ cake paraffin wax (2 oz.)
3 oz. white chocolate

In a double boiler melt milk chocolate chips, chocolate chips and paraffin wax. Blend completely. Dip strawberries in chocolate. Place on wax papered cookie sheets. For contrasting color, heat white chocolate so it is easy to drizzle with a small spoon over chocolate dipped strawberries. You can mix and match (as pictured), using milk, dark or white chocolate.

Fabulous Fudge ⚜

4 squares semi-sweet chocolate
1 tbsp. cream
8 oz. cream cheese
1 c. whole pecans
6 c. powered suger

Melt chocolate squares in microwave for 60-90 seconds stirring every 20 seconds until smooth. Add cream and cream cheese. Whip together. Slowly blend in cups of powered suger one at a time. Spread in a 9"x13" pan. Press pecans 1½" apart and refrigerate. Cut into squares and serve.

Coconut Cake ⚜

- 1 c. creamy butter
- 3 c. sugar
- 6 eggs
- 2 tsp. rich vanilla
- 1 tsp. coconut extract
- 2 tsp. baking powder
- 3½ c. flour
- 1 c. heavy cream

Preheat oven to 325°. Cream butter and sugar in mixing bowl. Add eggs, beat well until light and fluffy (1-2 minutes). Sift flour and baking powder into creamed mixture, alternating with whipping cream, mix well. Stir in coconut extract and vanilla. Spray three 9"round springform cake pans with cooking spray, evenly pour cake batter into each round pan and bake for 30-35 minutes or until toothpick comes out clean. This cake must be divided into three parts or it will not cook evenly. Remove cakes from springform pans. Quickly wrap cakes in plastic wrap to hold in moisture and let cool on a cooling rack or in refrigerator. When completely cooled, frost evenly with Buttercream Vanilla Frosting and top with generous amounts of fresh coconut.

Buttercream Vanilla Frosting ⚜

- 1 c. creamy butter
- 3 tsp. rich vanilla
- 8 c. powdered sugar
- ⅓ c. cream
- 2 c. shredded coconut

In small mixing bowl combine room temperature butter, cream and vanilla. Add powdered sugar to butter mixture. Whip until smooth. Frost first layer of cake, place second layer on top of frosted cake, frost. Place third layer on top and frost top and sides. Sprinkle frosted cake with two cups shredded coconut.

Coffee Pound Cream Cake ⚜

1 c. creamy butter	½ tsp. baking soda
3 c. sugar	1½ tsp. baking powder
6 fresh eggs	1 c. heavy whipping cream
3 tbsp. vegetable oil	1½ tsp. almond extract
3 c. flour	½ tsp. freshly ground nutmeg

Preheat oven to 350°. Cream together butter and sugar in a mixing bowl until light and fluffy. Add eggs and vegetable oil. Beat well. Add flour, baking soda and baking powder. Fold in whipping cream and mix well. Stir in almond extract and freshly ground nutmeg. Pour into greased 9"x 13" pan.

fresh nutmeg topping:

¾ c. creamy butter	1½ c. brown sugar
1 tsp. freshly ground nutmeg	½ tsp. cinnamon
¾ c. flour	

In a small mixing bowl, combine topping ingredients. Blend with fork until crumbly. Sprinkle over top of cake. Bake at 350° for 60-70 minutes. Topping will sink to bottom, turn baked cake onto a jelly roll pan and drizzle with Almond Butter Icing. Cut and serve.

Almond Butter Icing ⚜

¼ c. butter softened	2 c. powdered sugar
1½ tsp. almond extract	3 tbsp. cream

Blend all ingredients together until creamy. Cut cake to desired size and drizzle frosting over each piece.

Cream Cheese Brownies ⚜

1 c. semi-sweet chocolate chips

¼ c. unsweetened chocolate

1 c. + 2 tbsp. butter

4 lg. eggs

¼ tsp. salt

1 ½ tsp. vanilla extract

1¼ c. sugar

8 oz. softened cream cheese

⅓ c. sugar

½ tsp. vanilla extract

1 egg, yolk only

2 ¼ c. unsifted flour

Preheat oven to 325°. Melt semi-sweet and unsweetened chocolates with butter together in a double boiler and mix until smooth. Let the mixture cool to room temperature. In a separate bowl, gently mix eggs, salt, 1 ½ tsp. vanilla and 1¼ c. sugar until well blended. Do not whip. Whisk by hand to help prevent over-mixing. Blend in chocolate mixture. Sift the measured flour into the mixture and fold in with a spatula. Mix the softened cream cheese, ⅓ c. sugar, ½ tsp. vanilla extract and egg yolk together until smooth. Grease a jelly roll or sheet pan. Pour half of the brownie batter into the pan and spread it evenly. Then pour half of the cream cheese mixture in pools on top of the brownie mixture. Pour the remaining half of the brownie mixture over and spread evenly. Then scoop the remaining portion of the cream cheese mixture in pools on top. Swirl the two batters together slightly, using a butter knife. Bake for 25 minutes or until a toothpick inserted in the middle comes out clean.

Raspberry Truffles ⚜

truffle:

¼ c. + 1 tbsp. raspberry jam

½ c. heavy cream

½ c. creamy butter

3 c. semi-sweet chocolate chips

coating:

⅓ c. cocoa powder

⅓ c. powdered sugar

Bring the butter and whipping cream just to a simmer over medium heat. Reduce the heat, add the chocolate chips and whisk. Remove from heat and stir in the raspberry jam. Pour the mixture into a bowl and freeze 1 hour. Form into 1″ balls and set on lined cookie sheets. Refrigerate. Gently sift the cocoa powder and powdered sugar into a small bowl. Roll each truffle in the cocoa sugar mixture. Keep refrigerated until ready to serve.

Peanut Butter Balls ⚜

3 c. smooth peanut butter

¾ c. creamy butter

1½ lbs. powdered sugar

4½ c. Rice Krispies™

6 oz. semi-sweet chocolate chips

1 milk chocolate bar (10 oz.)

1 oz. paraffin wax

Mix peanut butter, butter and powdered sugar well. Add Rice Krispies™ and roll into balls. Chill. Melt paraffin wax and chocolate chips and chocolate bar in a double boiler or microwave. If using a microwave place chocolate in a glass bowl. Dip balls in melted chocolate and let cool on a cookie sheet lined with wax paper (for ease of cleanup). Serve.

Blueberry Coffee Cake ⚜

½ c. shortening

¾ c. sugar

1 egg

2 c. flour

2 ½ tsp. baking powder

¼ tsp. salt

¼ c. milk

¼ c. sour cream

2 c. fresh blueberries   ⅓ c. butter   1 c. light brown sugar   ¾ c. flour   ¾ tsp. cinnamon

Preheat oven to 350°. Cream shortening and sugar together. Add egg, beat well. Sift flour, baking powder and salt together. Fold into creamed mixture alternating with milk and sour cream. Put in a greased 10" pie pan or 9"x 9" pan. Sprinkle with blueberries. Cut butter, sugar, flour and cinnamon together until crumbly. Place on top of blueberries and bake for 45-50 minutes. Serve warm with whipped cream or your favorite vanilla ice cream.

Pumpkin Mousse ⚜

1 lg. box vanilla instant pudding mix (5.1 oz)

1¾ c. pure pumpkin (canned)

1⅔ c. sugar

1 can sweetened condensed milk (14 oz.)

1 tsp. freshly ground nutmeg

1½ tsp. pumpkin pie spice

2 c. heavy whipping cream

1 tsp. rich vanilla

Beat heavy whipping cream until stiff, add ⅔ c. sugar and 1 tsp. vanilla, set aside. In a large bowl combine pudding mix, pumpkin, 1 c. sugar, sweetened condensed milk, nutmeg and pumpkin pie spice. Fold in half of the whipped cream, blend completely. Using our Orange Ginger Snap Cookies or your favorite ginger snap cookie, break up cookies and place in bottom of goblet and spoon mousse over the top. Spread a thin layer of whipped cream, add another layer of crumbled cookies, spooning an additional layer of the pumpkin mousse. Finish with a dollop of whipped cream and top it off with a whole cookie.

Orange Ginger Snap Cookies ⚜

¾ c. vegetable shortening

1 c. dark brown sugar

½ c. molasses

1 egg

3 tbsp. finely grated orange rind

¾ tbsp. ground ginger

1 tsp. cinnamon

2 tsp. baking soda

2½ c. flour

orange sugar coating:

2 tbsp. finely grated orange rind

½ c. sugar

½ tsp. nutmeg

Preheat oven to 350°. Cream shortening, sugar and ginger until soft and fluffy. Beat in molasses and add egg, mixing well. Fold in orange rind. Separately sift together flour, cinnamon and baking soda. Stir into creamed mixture, blend thoroughly. In a small bowl, combine orange rind, sugar and nutmeg. Using half the dough, make balls no larger than the size of a quarter, keeping cookies small enough to fit inside goblets filled with Pumpkin Mousse. Using the remaining dough, make larger cookies to crumble in the bottom of the goblet. Roll balls of dough in sugar mixture. Place coated cookies on ungreased cookie sheet 3" apart. Bake for 10-12 minutes. Remove to cooling rack.

Raspberry Cheese Cake ⚜

crust:

3 c. graham cracker crumbs

¾ c. butter

½ c. sugar

Preheat oven to 325°. Mix dry ingredients together and blend with melted butter. Press into the bottom of a 9" deep pie tin. Bake in oven for 10-12 minutes. Refrigerate.

first layer of filling:

1 can sweetened condensed milk (14 oz.)

2 tbsp. lemon juice

8 oz. softened cream cheese

Whip sweetened condensed milk, cream cheese and lemon juice with an electric mixer until smooth. Pour into cooled graham cracker crust.

second layer of filling:

4 oz. softened cream cheese

½ c. powdered sugar

6 oz. sweetened condensed milk

1 tsp. lemon juice

¾ c. frozen raspberries

Blend cream cheese, powdered sugar, sweetened condensed milk and lemon juice together. With an electric mixer completely mix in ⅓ c. frozen raspberries. Add second layer to pie, chill. When ready to serve slice each piece and top with additional frozen raspberries. Cut and serve.

Coconut Balls ⚜

truffle:

½ c. creamy butter	12 oz. milk chocolate chips
½ c. heavy cream	½ c. fresh coconut
12 oz. semi-sweet chocolate chips	1 tsp. coconut extract

coating:

½ c. fresh coconut	2 c. powdered sugar

Bring the butter and heavy cream just to a simmer over medium heat. Reduce heat, add chocolate chips and whisk. Remove from heat and stir in fresh coconut and extract. Pour the mixture into a bowl and freeze 1 hour. Form into 1" balls with a melon baller and set on lined cookie sheet. Refrigerate. Gently mix the coconut and powdered sugar into a small bowl. Roll each truffle in the coconut and sugar mixture. Chill.

Crispy Peanut Butter Squares ⚜

½ c. Karo™ syrup

½ c. sugar

½ c. peanut butter

4 c. Rice Krispies™

2 c. milk or semi-sweet chocolate chips

Combine Karo™ syrup, sugar and peanut butter in microwave safe bowl and heat for 90 seconds, stirring every 30 seconds until smooth. Fold in Rice Krispies™, coating thoroughly and spread in a 9"x13" pan. Gently press for a smooth surface. Melt chocolate chips in microwave safe bowl for 1–1 ½ minutes, stirring every 20 seconds until smooth. Spread melted chocolate over Peanut Butter Squares and chill. Cut into desired size and serve.

Coconut Chex™ Mix ⚜

1½ c. butter
2 c. white sugar
2 c white Karo™ syrup
1 box of Corn Chex®
(14 oz. box)

1 box Golden Grahams™
(12 oz. box)
2 c. coconut
1½ c. slivered almonds

Preheat oven to 325°. Place slivered almonds on a cookie sheet and bake for 10-12 minutes. Set aside. In a large soup pot melt butter, add sugar and Karo™ syrup. Bring to a boil for 3 minutes. In a large bowl mix the toasted almonds, coconut, Corn Chex® and Golden Grahams™. Pour hot mixture over dry ingredients and spread on cookie sheets to cool.

Chocolate Almond Chex™ Mix ⚜

1½ c. butter
2 c. white sugar
2 c. white Karo™ syrup
1 box of Corn Chex®

1 box of Golden Grahams™
2 c. coconut
1½ c. whole salted almonds
2 c. white chocolate chips

Preheat oven to 325°. Chop whole salted almonds. Set aside. In a large soup pot melt butter, add sugar and Karo™ syrup. Bring to a boil for 3 minutes. Set aside. In a large bowl mix the chopped almonds, coconut, Corn Chex® and Golden Grahams™. Stir in 6 oz. of white chocolate chips. Mix evenly. Pour syrup over dry mix and coat evenly. As it cools add remaining chocolate chips. Stir together and spread on cookie sheet.

Butter Crisp Cookies ⚜

1 c. melted butter
2 c. brown sugar
4 c. oatmeal
2 tbsp. baking powder
1 tsp. salt
2 tsp. rich vanilla

dipping chocolate:

1 oz. paraffin wax   6 oz. chocolate chips
10 oz. milk chocolate bar

Preheat oven to 325°. Mix all ingredients well and spread in a jelly roll sheet pan, press down into the pan. Bake for 20-25 minutes. Remove from oven and quickly cut into desired shapes with cookie cutters, let cool.

Melt paraffin wax, milk chocolate bar and chocolate chips in a double boiler or micro-wave. Dip half of each cookie in the chocolate and place on wax paper. Let cool. Serve.

Peanut Butter Bars ⚜

1 c. creamy butter
1¼ c. peanut butter
1 c. sugar
1 c. brown sugar

2 lg. eggs
1 tsp. rich vanilla
1 tsp. baking soda

1 tsp. salt
2 c. flour
2 c. old fashioned oats

topping:

1½ c. peanut butter

1½ c. semi-sweet chocolate chips

Preheat oven to 350°. Cream together butter, peanut butter, sugar, brown sugar, eggs and vanilla. Stir in baking soda, salt and flour. Blend well. Fold in oats. Press a thin layer of dough into a jelly roll pan. Bake for 15 minutes. Remove from oven. Drop tablespoons of peanut butter over hot cookie. Sprinkle semi-sweet chocolate chips over top of hot cookie and let melt. With a spatula, spread peanut butter and melted chocolate chips over the entire pan like frosting. Let cool so chocolate and peanut butter firm up. Cut in squares and serve.

Banana Cream Pie ⚜

filling:

2 lg. box vanilla instant pudding (5.1 oz. ea.)

4 c. cold milk

2 c. heavy whipping cream

2 tsp. rich vanilla

1 c. sugar

6 large bananas

Beat pudding mix and cold milk with wire whisk until smooth. Refrigerate pudding while whipping the cream. Whip cream with electric hand mixer on high speed until peaks form. Fold in vanilla and sugar. Blend. Add two cups of whipped cream to the pudding mixture and fold together. Place sliced bananas along the bottom and the sides of the pie crust. Pour pudding over bananas and fill pie crust. Spread remaining whipped cream on top of filling. Refrigerate and serve.

Pie Crust ⚜

2 c. flour   1 tsp. salt   ¾ c. shortening   6–7 tbsp. ice water   1 egg white

Prepare pie crust first. Preheat oven to 450°. Sift flour and salt together, cut in shortening with pastry blender until pieces are the size of small peas. Sprinkle ice water over dry mixture, gently blend together. Turn onto a floured surface, handling as little as possible. Divide dough in half, gently roll out pastry to fit pie dish. Line pie dish, flute edges and prick pastry with fork. Lightly beat egg white and brush fluted edges. Bake at 450° for 10–12 minutes or until golden. Makes two 8–9" pie crusts.

Notes & Comments

❧ Quick References ❧

A pinch = ⅛ teaspoon or less

3 teaspoons = 1 tablespoon

4 tablespoons = ¼ cup

5⅓ tablespoons = ⅓ cup

8 tablespoons = ½ cup

10 ⅔ tablespoons = ⅔ cup

12 tablespoons = ¾ cup

16 tablespoons = 1 cup

1 ounce = 28.35 grams

1 pound = 435.59 grams

1 gram = 0.0335 ounces

1 kilogram = 2.2 pounds

1 tablespoon = ½ fluid ounce

1 cup = 8 fluid ounces

1 cup = ½ pint

2 cups = 1 pint

4 cups = 1 quart

2 pints = 1 quart

4 quarts = 1 gallon

8 quarts = 1 peck

2 gallons = 1 peck

4 pecks = 1 bushel

1 tablespoon = 14.79 milliliters

1 cup = 236.6 milliliters

1 quart = 946.4 milliliters

1 liter = 1.06 quarts

Measurements & Cooking References

Cooking Temperatures

beef............................. 140°........................... rare

beef............................. 160°...................... medium

beef............................. 170°.................. well-done

pork .... 165°......................... done

ham, precooked .... 140°....................... done

chicken, whole .... 175°......................... done

turkey, whole .... 180°......................... done

stuffing .... 165°......................... done

poultry parts .... 170°......................... done

Oven Temperature

225° – 275° .... Very Slow

300° – 325° .... Slow

350° – 375°.................................. Moderate

400° – 425° .... Hot

450° – 475° .... Extremely Hot

500° – 550° .... Broiling

Liquid conversions

1 gal.	4 qt.	8 pt.	16 c.	128 fl. oz.	3.79 L		
1/2 gal.	2 qt.	4 pt.	8 c.	64 fl oz.	1.89 L		
1/4 gal.	1 qt.	2 pt.	4 c.	32 fl oz.	.95 L		
	½ qt.	1 pt.	2 c.	16 fl oz.	.47 L		
	¼ qt.	½ pt.	1 c.	8 fl oz.	.24 L		
			½ c.	4 fl oz.	.12 L	8 tbsp.	24 tsp.
			1/4 c	2 fl oz.	.06 L	4 tbsp.	12 tsp.
			⅛. c.	1 fl oz.	.03 L	2 tbsp.	6 tsp.
				½ fl oz.	.015 L	1 tbsp.	3 tsp.

Dry Measure conversions

1 c.	8 fl oz.	16 tbsp.	48 tsp.	237 ml
¾ c.	6 fl oz.	12 tbsp.	36 tsp.	177 ml
⅔ c.	5⅓ fl oz.	10⅔ tbsp.	32 tsp.	158 ml
½ c.	4 fl oz.	8 tbsp.	24 tsp.	118 ml
⅓ c.	2⅔ fl oz.	5⅓ tbsp.	16 tsp.	79 ml
¼ c.	2 fl oz.	4 tbsp	12 tsp.	59 ml
⅛ c.	1 fl oz.	2 tbsp	6 tsp.	30 ml
1/16 c.	½ fl oz.	1 tbsp.	3 tsp.	15 ml
1/48 c.	⅛ fl oz.	⅓ tbsp.	1 tsp.	5 ml

Index

A

Aged Balsamic Vinaigrette........................57
Aged Red Wine Dressing............................89
Almond Butter Icing.................................202
Almond Tuna Cheddar Melt........................18

Appetizers

Avocado Egg Roll...................................124
Bacon Tater Tots™..................................154
Barbecue Chicken Pizza...........................156
Basil Tomato Bites.................................154
Chicken Wing Fling.................................152
Gorgonzola Cheese Spread..........................32
Guacamole Shrimp...................................155
Herbed Parmesan Crisps............................161
Island Salsa.......................................153
Mango Salsa..160
Oven Roasted Cinnamon Crisps......................161
Oven Roasted Sesame Cheese........................157
Pastry Wrapped Sausages...........................119
Pot stickers......................................123
Potato Sundae Bar..................................158
Shrimp Ceviche.....................................153
Stuffed Mushrooms..................................155
Sweet Berry Rosemary Flat Bread...................150

Artichoke Delight...................................52
Asiago Potato Soup..................................19
Asian Chicken Salad................................122
Asparagus Wild Rice.................................39
Avocado Egg Rolls.................................124

B

Baby Basil Potatoes...............................113
Baby Red Mashed Potatoes......................71, 158
Bacon Bow Tie Salad................................51
Bacon Chicken Pasta...............................141
Bacon Potato Salad................................187
Bacon Sugar Snap Peas.............................113
Bacon Tater Tots™.................................154
Baja Steamed Rice..................................13
Balsamic Cheese Dressing...........................99
Banana Cream Pie..................................214
Barbecue Chicken Pizza............................156
Barbecue Chicken Salad............................181
Barbecue Chicken Sauce............................181
Barbecue Sauce....................................128
Basil Tomato Bites................................154

Beef

Beef Broccoli.....................................167
Beef Stroganoff,..................................145
Favorite Meat Ball Spaghetti.......................56
Ginger Beef Soup..................................173
Ginger Glazed Kabobs...............................70
Gorgonzola Crusted Beef Tenderloin.................44
Maggie's Marinated Burgers........................128
Rib Eye Pot Pie...................................104
Shepherd's Pie....................................142
Traditional Chili.................................170
Tri Tip Steak......................................30

Beef Broccoli.....................................167

Beef Stroganoff...................................145
Beet Salad...41
Biscuit Dough.....................................140
Bleu Cheese Potato Chips..........................130
Blueberry Coffee Cake.............................205
Blueberry Torte...................................199
Boston Brown Bread.................................65

Breads and Rolls

Biscuit Dough.....................................140
Boston Brown Bread.................................65
Cheese Crusted Croutons............................21
Chocolate Banana Bread............................107
Cornbread from the Heart...........................14
Feta Cheese Toast..................................72
Focaccia Bread.....................................58
Herb Roasted Flat Bread...........................150
Honey Glazed Walnut Rolls..........................40
Rosemary Bread.....................................90
Savory Cheddar Biscuits............................26
Shelley's Famous Scones...........................114
Sweet Stuffed French Toast.........................77
Sweet Tomato Basil Bread..........................100
Toasted Cheese Bread...............................95
Whole Wheat Mini Loaves............................46
Zucchini Bread....................................107

Broccoli Souffle...................................95
Butter Crisp Cookies..............................212
Butter Tarts......................................197
Buttercream Vanilla Frosting......................201
Butternut Squash...................................39

C

Cakes

Blueberry Coffee Cake 205
Coconut Cake 201
Coffee Pound Cream Cake 202
Cream Cheese Brownies 203
Mini Carrot Bundt Cake 196

Candied Pecan Salad 73
Candied Walnuts 178,183

Candy

Chocolate Almond Chex™ Mix 211
Coconut Balls 209
Coconut Chex™ Mix 211
Fabulous Fudge 200
Peanut Butter Balls 204
Raspberry Truffles 204

Carrots and Sugar Snap Peas 71
Cheese Crusted Croutons 21

Chicken

Asian Chicken Salad 122
Bacon Chicken Pasta 141
Barbecue Chicken Pizza 156
Barbecue Chicken Salad 181
Chicken a la King 137
Chicken Barley 174
Chicken Cordon Bleu 38
Chicken Crepes 118
Chicken Pita Sandwiches 50
Chicken Pot Pie 105
Chicken Rosemary 138

Chicken Stir Fry Soup 172
Chicken Stroganoff 94
Chicken Tetrazzini 146
Chicken Vegetable Stir Fry 144
Chicken Wing Fling 152
Chicken Wonton Salad 182
Crispy Chicken Avocado Tacos 12
Harvest Chicken and Yams 64
Heavenly Chicken Curry 143
Home Style Chicken Chili 168
Oriental Chicken Salad 180
Rosemary Chicken 151
Spicy Honey Glazed Chicken 24
Sweet and Sour Chicken 82
Three Cheese Chicken Tortellini 165
Waldorf Chicken Salad 178

Chicken a la King 137
Chicken Barley 174
Chicken Cordon Bleu 38
Chicken Crepes 118
Chicken Pita Sandwiches 50
Chicken Pot Pie 105
Chicken Rosemary 138
Chicken Stir Fry Soup 172
Chicken Stroganoff 94
Chicken Tetrazzini 146
Chicken Vegetable Stir Fry 144
Chicken Wing Fling 152
Chicken Wonton Salad 182
Chocolate Almond Chex™ Mix 211
Chocolate Banana Bread 107
Chocolate Dipped Strawberries 200
Chocolate Crisp Cupcakes 198
Cilantro Lime Dipping Sauce 124

Coconut Balls 209
Coconut Cake 201
Coconut Chex™ Mix 211
Coffee Pound Cream Cake 202
Cream of Mushroom 164

Cookies and Bars

Butter Crisp Cookies 212
Cream Cheese Brownies 203
Crispy Peanut Butter Squares 210
Orange Ginger Snap Cookies 207
Peanut Butter Bars 213
Star Cookie Crunch 195

Cornbread from the Heart 14
Cream Cheese Brownies 203
Cream Cheese Frosting 196
Cream of Mushroom 164
Creamy Cilantro Dressing 187
Crepes 118
Crimson Grape Salad 66
Crispy Chicken Avocado Tacos 12
Crispy Peanut Butter Squares 210
Crunchy Cucumber Salad 33

D

Date Salad 94
Dill Dressing 51

Desserts

Banana Cream Pie 214
Blueberry Coffee Cake 205
Blueberry Torte 199
Butter Crisp Cookies 212
Butter Tarts 197

Chocolate Crisp Cupcakes 198
Chocolate Dipped Strawberries 200
Coconut Cake...201
Coffee Pound Cream Cake.........................202
Cream Cheese Brownies 203
Crispy Peanut Butter Squares 210
Mini Carrot Bundt Cake.............................196
Orange Ginger Snap Cookies.................... 207
Oreo™ Chocolate Banana Cream Pie..........194
Peanut Butter Bars.................................... 213
Pumpkin Mousse....................................... 206
Raspberry Cheese Cake............................. 208
Star Cookie Crunch 195

Dressings
see salad dressings................................223

F
Fabulous Fudge 200
Favorite Meat Ball Spaghetti 56
Feta Cheese Toast..72
Focaccia Bread..58
French Tomato Soup 166
Fresh Pesto..57
Fruit Glaze 78
Fruit Medley 78

Frostings
Almond Butter Icing..................................202
Buttercream Vanilla Frosting 201
Cream Cheese Frosting 196
Dipping Chocolate..................................... 212

Fruits
Chocolate Dipped Strawberries 200

Fruit Medley 78
Spring Mix Fruit Salad 183
Strawberry Greens 47
Strawberry Kiwi Salad 115
Strawberry Spinach Salad 20

G
Garden Fresh Rice.......................................25
German Fries...32
Ginger Beef Soup.......................................173
Ginger Glaze 112
Ginger Glazed Kabobs................................70
Ginger Glazed Salmon 112

Glazes
Fruit Glaze 78
Honey Walnut Glaze 40
Ginger Glaze 112

Glazed Long Grain Rice 45
Gorgonzola Cheese Spread 32
Gorgonzola Crusted Beef Tenderloin 44
Gorgonzola Ranch Dressing 179
Guacamole Shrimp......................................155

H
Harvest Chicken and Yams.........................64
Heavenly Chicken Curry 143
Herbed Parmesan Crisps 161
Herb Roasted Flat Bread 150
Homemade Ranch Dressing 188
Homemade Dry Ranch Dressing Mix 188
Home Style Chicken Chili........................... 168
Honey Dijon Vinaigrette 41
Honey Glazed Walnut Rolls 40

Honey Mustard Dressing 20
Honey Walnut Glaze 40
Hot Sauce..136

I
Island Salsa..153
Italian Lasagna Sauce 98
Italian Shrimp Pasta 88
Italian Style Chop Salad 89

J
Jalapeño Hamburger Salsa 129

M
Maggie's Marinated Burgers 128
Mango Salsa...160
Mashed Sweet Potatoes.............................159

Main Dishes
Bacon Chicken Pasta 145
Barbecue Chicken Pizza.............................156
Beef Stroganoff..145
Chicken a la King 137
Chicken Cordon Bleu...................................38
Chicken Crepes 118
Chicken Pot Pie 105
Chicken Rosemary 138
Chicken Stroganoff 94
Chicken Tetrazzini 146
Chicken Vegetable Stir Fry.........................144
Crispy Chicken Avocado Tacos 12
Favorite Meat Ball Spaghetti 56
Ginger Glazed Kabobs................................70
Ginger Glazed Salmon 112
Gorgonzola Crusted Beef Tenderloin........ 44

Harvest Chicken and Yams....................64
Heavenly Chicken Curry.......................143
Home Style Chicken Chili.....................168
Italian Shrimp Pasta..............................88
Karl's Famous Breakfast Burritos........136
Maggie's Marinated Burgers................128
Pulled Pork Quesadilla.........................139
Rib Eye Pot Pie....................................104
Rosemary Chicken...............................151
Sausage Biscuits and Gravy.................140
Sausage Potato Cakes............................76
Shepherd's Pie.....................................142
Spicy Honey Glazed Chicken.................24
Sweet and Sour Chicken........................82
Sweet Stuffed French Toast....................77
Traditional Chili..................................170
Traditional Lasagna...............................98
Tri Tip Steak..30

Mini Carrot Bundt Cake.......................196
Mozzarella Salad....................................57
Mozzarella Spinach Salad....................131

N

Nine Layer Salad....................................27

Nuts

Candied Walnuts..........................178,183
Oven Roasted Sweet Pecans.................159
Sweet Walnuts......................................151

O

Orange Ginger Snap Cookies...............207
Orange Lime Dressing..........................115

Oreo™ Chocolate Banana Cream Pie....194
Oriental Chicken Salad.........................180
Oven Roasted Cinnamon Crisps..........161
Oven Roasted Sesame Cheese..............157
Oven Roasted Sweet Pecans.................159
Oven Roasted Sweet Potato Fries...........21

P

Parmesan Baked Veggies........................25
Pastry Wrapped Sausages.....................119
Pastry.........................104,105,119,197,214
Peanut Butter Balls..............................204
Peanut Butter Bars...............................213
Peanut Ginger Dressing.......................182

Pies, Tarts and Tortes

Banana Cream Pie................................214
Blueberry Torte....................................199
Butter Tarts..197
Oreo™ Chocolate Banana Cream pie....194

Pork

Pulled Pork Quesadilla.........................139

Pot Stickers..123
Potato Bacon Soup...............................169
Potato Sundae Bar...............................158
Pulled Pork Quesadilla.........................139
Pumpkin Mousse.................................206

R

Raspberry Cheese Cake........................208
Raspberry Truffles................................204
Red Wine Peppercorn Dressing.............47

Rib Eye Pot Pie....................................104
Roasted Barley.......................................65
Rosemary Bread.....................................90
Rosemary Chicken...............................151

S
Salads

Asian Chicken Salad.............................122
Bacon Bow Tie Salad..............................51
Bacon Potato Salad..............................187
Barbecue Chicken Salad.......................181
Beet Salad..41
Candied Pecan Salad..............................73
Chicken Wonton Salad.........................182
Crimson Grape Salad.............................66
Crunchy Cucumber Salad......................33
Date Salad..94
Italian Style Chop Salad.........................89
Mozzarella Salad....................................57
Mozzarella Spinach Salad....................131
Nine Layer Salad....................................27
Oriental Chicken Salad.........................180
Santa Fe Salad......................................184
Shrimp Cauliflower Salad.......................13
Spinach and Bell Pepper Salad..............99
Spinach and Mushroom Salad..............106
Spring Mix Fruit Salad.........................183
Spring Shrimp Salad.............................186
Strawberry Greens..................................47
Strawberry Kiwi Salad..........................115
Strawberry Spinach Salad.......................20
Tortellini Turkey Salad.........................179
Turkey Penne Salad..............................185
Waldorf Chicken Salad.........................178

Salsa

Island Salsa 153
Jalapeño Hamburger Salsa 129
Mango Salsa 160
Spicy Salsa Ranch 12

Salad Dressings

Aged Balsamic Vinaigrette 57
Aged Red Wine Dressing 89
Balsamic Cheese Dressing 99
Creamy Cilantro Dressing 187
Dill Dressing 51
Gorgonzola Ranch Dressing 179
Homemade Ranch Dressing 188
Honey Dijon Vinaigrette 41
Honey Mustard Dressing 20
Orange Lime Dressing 115
Peanut Ginger Dressing 182
Red Wine Peppercorn Dressing 47
Spicy Salsa Ranch 12
Sweet Apple Cider Dressing 106
Sweet Balsamic 183
Sweet Basil Dressing 131
Sweet Jalapeño Cilantro Dressing 184
Sweet Onion Dijon Dressing 178
Sweet Onion Dressing 186
Sweet Poppy Seed Dressing 73
Sweet Sesame Dressing 180
Toasted Sesame Dressing 122
Zesty Lime Dressing 185

Sandwiches

Almond Tuna Cheddar Melt 18
Chicken Pita Sandwiches 50

Santa Fe Salad 184
Sausage Biscuits and Gravy 140
Sausage Potato Cakes 76
Sausage Vegetable Orzo 171
Savory Cheddar Biscuits 26
Savory Mushroom Stock 83

Sauces

Barbecue Chicken Sauce 181
Barbecue Sauce 128
Cilantro Lime Dipping Sauce 124
Fresh Pesto 57
Hot Sauce 136
Italian Lasagna Sauce 98
Teriyaki Marinade 30
Tuscan Marinara Sauce 56

Sausage

Karl's Famous Breakfast Burritos 136
Pastry Wrapped Sausages 119
Pot Stickers 123
Sausage Biscuits and Gravy 140
Sausage Potato Cakes 76
Sausage Vegetable Orzo 171
Stuffed Zucchini 31

Seafood

Almond Tuna Cheddar Melt 18
Ginger Glazed Salmon 112
Guacamole Shrimp 155
Italian Shrimp Pasta 88
Shrimp Cauliflower Salad 13
Shrimp Ceviche 153
Spring Shrimp Salad 186

Shelley's Famous Scones 114
Shelley's Honey Butter 114
Shepherd's Pie 142
Shrimp Cauliflower Salad 13
Shrimp Ceviche 153

Side Dishes

Artichoke Delight 52
Asparagus Wild Rice 39
Avocado Egg Rolls 124
Baby Basil Potatoes 113
Baby Red Mashed Potatoes 71,158
Bacon Sugar Snap Peas 113
Baja Steamed Rice 13
Bleu Cheese Potato Chips 130
Broccoli Souffle 95
Butternut Squash 39
Carrots and Sugar Snap Peas 71
Garden Fresh Rice 25
German Fries 32
Glazed Long Grain Rice 45
Mashed Sweet Potatoes 159
Oven Roasted Sweet Potato Fries 21
Parmesan Baked Veggies 25
Pastry Wrapped Sausages 119
Pot Stickers 123
Potato Sundae Bar 158
Roasted Barley 65
Steamed Asparagus 66
Stuffed Mushrooms 155
Stuffed Zucchini 31
Toasted Sesame Asparagus 129
White Wine Brussels Sprouts 45

Soups

Asiago Potato Soup......19
Beef Broccoli......167
Chicken Barley......174
Chicken Stir Fry Soup......172
Cream of Mushroom......164
French Tomato Soup......166
Ginger Beef Soup......173
Home Style Chicken Chili......168
Potato Bacon Soup......169
Sausage Vegetable Orzo......171
Savory Mushroom Stock......83
Three Cheese Chicken Tortellini......165
Traditional Chili......170

Spreads

Gorgonzola Cheese Spread......32
Shelley's Honey Butter......114
Sweet Berry Spread......151

Sparkling Limeade......14
Spicy Honey Glazed Chicken......24
Spicy Salsa Ranch......12
Spinach and Bell Pepper Salad......99
Spinach and Mushroom Salad......106
Spring Mix Fruit Salad......183
Spring Shrimp Salad......186
Star Cookie Crunch......195
Steamed Asparagus......66
Stir Fried Vegetables......83
Strawberry Greens......47
Strawberry Kiwi Salad......115
Strawberry Spinach Salad......20
Stuffed Mushrooms......155

Stuffed Zucchini......31
Sweet and Sour Chicken......82
Sweet Apple Cider Dressing......106
Sweet Balsamic......183
Sweet Basil Dressing......131
Sweet Berry Rosemary Flat Bread......150
Sweet Berry Spread......151
Sweet Jalapeño Cilantro Dressing......184
Sweet Onion Dijon Dressing......178
Sweet Onion Dressing......186
Sweet Poppy Seed Dressing......73
Sweet Sesame Dressing......180
Sweet Stuffed French Toast......77
Sweet Tomato Basil Bread......100
Sweet Walnuts......151

T

Teriyaki Marinade......30
Three Cheese Chicken Tortellini......165
Toasted Cheese Bread......95
Toasted Sesame Asparagus......129
Toasted Sesame Dressing......122
Tortellini Turkey Salad......179
Traditional Chili......170
Traditional Lasagna......98
Tri Tip Steak......30
Turkey Penne Salad......185
Tuscan Marinara Sauce......56

Turkey

Turkey Penne Salad......185
Tortellini Turkey Salad......179

Vegetables

Artichoke Delight......52
Asparagus Wild Rice......39
Baby Basil Potatoes......113
Baby Red Mashed Potatoes......71,158
Bacon Sugar Snap Peas......113
Beef Broccoli......167
Bleu Cheese Potato Chips......130
Broccoli Souffle......95
Butternut Squash......39
Carrots and Sugar Snap Peas......71
Chicken Vegetable Stir Fry......144
German Fries......32
Harvest Chicken and Yams......64
Mashed Sweet Potatoes......159
Oven Roasted Sweet Potato Fries......21
Parmesan Baked Veggies......25
Potato Sundae Bar......158
Sausage Vegetable Orzo......171
Steamed Asparagus......66
Stir Fried Vegetables......83
Stuffed Mushrooms......155
Stuffed Zucchini......31
Toasted Sesame Asparagus......129
White Wine Brussels Sprouts......45

W

Waldorf Chicken Salad......178
White Wine Brussels Sprouts......45
Whole Wheat Mini Loaves......46

Z

Zesty Lime Dressing......185
Zucchini Bread......107

❧ Acknowledgements ❧

Thanks to our very talented graphic designer Brayden Iwasaki for long hours working with girls, girls, girls!

Thanks to Megan Cornelius Turley, our photographer who made every shoot a pleasure.

Thanks to Jean Olsen for giving it her all.

Thanks to Kara Listen for her keen eyes and generous sound advice.

Thanks to my son Abraham for his literary talents.

A special thanks to my husband Kenny and my beautiful daughters Abby Jane, Rachael, Maggie, Grace and Chloé who labored long and hard to contribute to this dream.

Thank you to Thanksgiving Point and
Details for generously sharing their tableware.

A special thanks to those who shared their unique gifts and talents:

Tyson and Abby Jane Green	Judi Bourne	Vicki Neeleman
Spencer and Rachael Crittenden	Bobbi Green	WC Wells
Ryan and Maggie Fish	Lauren Rudd	Denise Fielding
Abraham Taylor	Brooke Bowers	Jean Olsen
Jewels Rasmussen	Jhordan Cox	Stac'ey Volden
Sharee C, Paulson	Lori Miller Haugen	Lori Harper
Jim Clark	Shirley Haugen	Shelley Frampton
Richard Bickerton	Torri Moncivais	Karl Birkeland
June Bickerton	Heidi Allen	Grace and Chloé Huxtable
Pat Fish	Bobbi Smith	Kenneth John Huxtable Jr.

AMBphotocompany.com

Michelle Huxtable has successfully created gathering places for many years as an interior designer. Her passion for creating a comfortable and inviting atmosphere is motivated by her innate desire to surround herself and others with beauty. She derives great joy from gathering her family and friends around her because she feels that food is a love language and that lovingly preparing a meal is a genuine expression of one's self. Michelle has owned an interior design firm for over 20 years. She also enjoys working with her husband in the construction industry. She has six children and five grandchildren. They reside in Holladay, Utah.

The Gathering of Friends Volume Two: Let's Make Food Your Love Language was created by Michelle Huxtable with the help of her daughters: Abby Jane Green, Rachael Crittenden, Maggie Fish and Grace and Chlo'e Huxtable. They each share a love for creating savory recipes and especially gathering together to celebrate life.

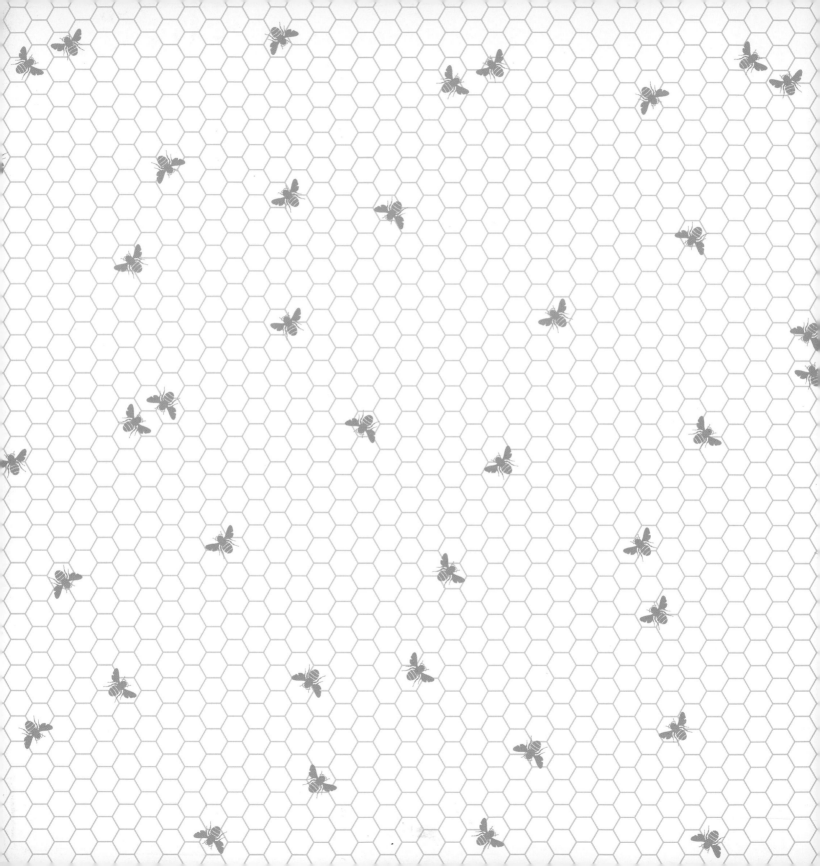

The Gathering

Volume Three

of Friends

Friends Favorites

Share your treasured memories along with your favorite keepsake recipes and become part of our third book from The Gathering of Friends series: *"Friends Favorites"*

Your "Friends Favorite" recipe entry should include:

- ❧ Name, address and phone number.
- ❧ Recipe with detailed instructions.
- ❧ Story behind your recipe to be included in Volume Three.
- ❧ A photo of your prepared recipe with your entry information attached.
- ❧ Mail your "Friends Favorite" to: Clarenden Woods, LLC

  5072 South Clarenden Pl.

  Holladay, Utah 84117

  or email your entries to: thegatheringoffriends@gmail.com

If your recipe is chosen you will receive a complimentary copy of *The Gathering of Friends Volume Three, Friends Favorites.*